WISDOM RIVER

MEDITATIONS ON FLY FISHING

AND LIFE MIDSTREAM

WISDOM RIVER

MEDITATIONS ON FLY FISHING AND LIFE MIDSTREAM

EDITORS: LARRY KAPUSTKA PHD
CHAD OKRUSCH PHD

FOREWORD: GREG SHYBA

UPROUTE IMPRINT OF DURVILE & UPROUTE BOOKS
CALGARY, ALBERTA, CANADA
DURVILE.COM

Durvile Publications Ltd.

UPROUTE IMPRINT OF DURVILE AND UPROUTE BOOKS

Calgary, Alberta, Canada
www.durvile.com

LIBRARY AND ARCHIVES CATALOGUING IN PUBLICATIONS DATA

Wisdom River: Meditations on Fly Fishing and Life Midstream
Kapustka, Larry: Editor
Okrusch, Chad: Editor
Shyba, Greg: Foreword

1. Fly Fishing | 2. Trout | 3. Montana | 4. Alberta
5. Meditation | 6. Sports and Recreation

The UpRoute Every River Lit Series

ISBN: 978-1-990735-11-0 (print pbk) | 978-1-990735-47-9 (e-pub)
978-1-990735-46-2 (audio)

Kayla Lappin's story "The Veil" also appears in the book,
Embrace Your Divine Flow, Durvile, 2023.

Jacket Cover Photograph: Tim Foster of Dose Media for Wild Valley Supply Co.
Book design: Lorene Shyba

We acknowledge the traditional land of the Treaty 7 Peoples of Southern Alberta: the Siksika, Piikani, and Kainai of the Niisitapi (Blackfoot) Confederacy; the Dene Tsuut'ina; and the Chiniki, Bearspaw, and Wesley Stoney Nakoda First Nations and the Region 3 Métis Nation of Alberta.

Durvile Publications gratefully acknowledges the financial support of The Government of Canada through Canadian Heritage Canada Book Fund and The Government of Alberta, Alberta Media Fund.

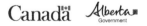

For fly fishers of all ages.

May all your fish be bigger

than the holes in your net.

WISDOM RIVER

CONTENTS

Foreword, *Esprit de corps*, Greg Shyba 9

Introduction, Water,
Larry Kapustka & Chad Okrusch................... 13

1. Almost Montana, Jim McLennan........................... 17

2. Waiting for Iris, Kaitlyn Okrusch........................... 23

3. As Good As Gold, Pat Munday 31

4. Poems and Musings, Doris Daley, Al (Doc) Mehl,
   Larry Kapustka, Chad Okrusch............................... 43

5. The Veil, Kayla Lappin............................... 59

6. Whenever I Close My Eyes, Jerry Kustich 77

7. Pardners and Dogs, Paul Vang................................ 91

8. Gallery, Photos by Tim Foster 101

9. How You Fellas Making Out? Greg Allard........... 113

10. A Love Story, David McCumber 125

WISDOM RIVER

CONTENTS

11. There's This Canadian Guy, Chris Pibus 135

12. The Total Fishing Experience,
    Line to Table & Recipes, Larry Kapustka 147

13. His River Teachings, Rayelynn Brandt 167

14. The Art of Raising Kids on the Big Hole
    Without Fishing, John McKee 185

Appendix of Dad's Fishing Jokes 191
About the Poets & Artists 199
About the Editors and Foreword Author 200

ESPRIT DE CORPS

Greg Shyba

I have never seen a river that I could not love.
Moving water...has a fascinating vitality.
It has power and grace and associations.
It has a thousand colors and a thousand shapes,
yet it follows laws so definite that the tiniest streamlet
is an exact replica of a great river.
— *Roderick Haig-Brown*

I HOPE YOU ENJOY this collection of stories about rivers and the varied interactions depicted. Fly fishing in many of the essays is a vehicle to express a reverence for the many gifts we receive along and in the rivers and cricks. As a fellow fly fishing enthusiast, I am pleased to see this outstanding collection go to print with each chapter being a reflection of the pleasures, challenges and life lessons found in time spent on rivers.

My own lifelong enthusiasm for fishing began when I was around five years old on trips to the famous Blue Ribbon Bow River east of Calgary with my dad. Now, fishing with my own kids and grandkids has become an important part of my family's culture and, in my case, it led me to a career in conservation.

Within these pages, the reader will find stories that catch the essence of fly fishing: the rise, the take and bringing a fish to hand but, most of all, being in close touch with nature. For many anglers, the concentration required to be successful takes their minds away from the stress in their lives. I know of several fly fishers whose love of the sport has taken priority over their jobs and families in their pursuit of the wily trout.

Although fly fishing is a solitary activity which lends itself to introspection, there is a certain *esprit de corps* shared by fly fishers. It is something organic that can be found deep within the soul of fly fishers. I have seen and been part of life-long relationships spawned from the love of fly fishing. I believe it is deeper than that of other sports or hobbies. And as they say, a lot of time is spent, planning and discussing what it will take to fool a fish with a brain the size of a pea.

Fly fishing can be exciting and disappointing when the angler can't "match the hatch," although some anglers will study the water for hours without casting a line, hoping to make that one cast in the hope that the weight of a fish will be on the line, even if for only a moment. Others I have fished with will stay on the water long into the night muttering to themselves and others, "Just one more cast!"

As this collection of stories reflects, not only anglers enjoy time spent on rivers. Others, such as bird watchers and those drifting by on a canoe, also enjoy viewing

Greg Shyba with framed fly fishing memorabilia
from boyhood fishing trips.

---

all that nature offers on or along its riverbanks. It has
been said that to protect a river, it needs many friends.
As you read through the book, I am sure you will recognize the passion of these writers through their unique
account of experiences on their water.

Tight lines and happy reading!

—*Greg Shyba, CEO,*
Ann & Sandy Cross Conservation Area,
Calgary, Alberta 2023

WATER

Larry Kapustka and Chad Okrusch

Dr. Larry Kapustka
Diamond Valley, Alberta

Dr. Chad Okrusch
Butte, Montana

W ATER IS PRECIOUS, essential for life, and inspirational. We are drawn to rivers and lakes not just for the basic needs of survival, but also for recreational and spiritual replenishment, a calming of our psyche, an opportunity to encounter nature in all its glory. The motion of water can be mesmerizing, whether the turbulent flow over cataracts or the soothing flow in a deep pool. When one is on the water, the chance encounter with Brother Bear, a timid fawn, or a soaring osprey builds everlasting memories.

Even though the water that flows in streams and rivers represents a mere 0.002 percent of Earth's water, it plays an outsized role for most of us. While one can feel the energy of the sun and hear the wind shake quaking aspen leaves, there is something about struggling to stand firm in the onrush of moving water as it works its way downstream that makes the earth's energy palpable in a singular way.

The magic of moving water and the animals that reside in streams and rivers is the source of inspiration for the collection of stories and poems in this book. The authors bring together a richness of experiences, some drawing life lessons gained from being knee-deep in flowing waters. Many stories focus on fly fishing for trout, but like Norman Maclean's "A River Runs Through It," the act of fly fishing is merely a vehicle to tell deeper stories.

We open with Jim McLennan's tribute to esteemed fly fishing experts who wrote eloquently about the blue-ribbon trout streams of Montana that compelled mostly boys and young men to dream of the day they would ply these magical places. As Jim tells of his journey, one is led to conclude that there are other places, other rivers that yield larger and more trout than the revered Montana streams. Yet, the aura that surrounds the iconic Montana Rivers prevails. This theme returns in the memories shared by Chris Pibus and David McCumber.

A common thread that emerges from all the authors, even those who focused on the art of fly fishing, is that time on the water evokes much more that landing a beautiful cuttie, bow, brook, or brown. There are echos of John Denver's "serenity of a clear blue mountain lake" in the poems by Doc Mehl and Doris Daley. There are stories in essays by Pat Munday and poems by Doc and Doris of precious natural resources lost to greed and arrogance. There are also hopeful expressions in the story about Iris, a resident osprey, by Kaitlynn Okrusch. There are poignant love stories recounted by Kayla Lappin, Paul Vang, Jerry Kustich,

David McCumber, and John McKee—each linked to adventures on streams. Beyond the life's lessons shared in these tales, there are suggestions for your next dining experience with recipes for the rivershore campfire and for elegant dining room table spreads.

The stories told in this book are drawn from Alberta and Montana, with a photography gallery of images by Tim Foster from Nova Scotia. Artwork by Tyler Rock (glass bull trout), additional photos by Mike Forbister, and chapter heading drawings by Rich Théroux provide depth to this production.

Wisdom River is both real and imagined—a metaphor that draws in precious memories and inspirations. The real place, shown on maps as the "Big Hole" in Montana, was initially named "Wisdom River" in 1806 by Lewis and Clark, who were commissioned by Thomas Jefferson to find a water route to the Pacific Ocean.

Wisdom Rivers exist wherever we are learning on their banks—the Tigris and the Nile; the Columbia and the Amazon; the Mackenzie, the McKenzie and the Bow—all are Wisdom Rivers. Every headwater stream, every Fish, Willow, and Rock Creek brings wisdom. Most of the work herein was inspired by fishing for trout. Sometimes the fishers are fly fishing, sometimes they're fish hawks, and in at least one chapter no one is fishing at all.

—*Larry Kapustka, Diamond Valley, Alberta*
Chad Okrusch, Butte, Montana
2023

ONE

ALMOST MONTANA

Jim McLennan

Mystique:
"A quality of mystery, glamour, or power associated
with someone or something."

IT WAS AROUND 1965 when my parents announced we would be taking a fishing trip from our home in Alberta to meet up with a couple of my dad's old school pals whom he hadn't seen in fifty or so years. The trip was to Cooke City, Montana, just outside the northeast corner of Yellowstone Park.

We fished some streams nearby, including the Lamar River and Slough Creek in the Park, dangling worms behind a lead weight. We cast into the moving water and let the worms hang in the current near an undercut bank till a trout took hold. The fish, cutthroats, I seem to remember, were taken back to the motel, fried up, and enjoyed.

Though this trip included little or no fly fishing, it came along at a time when I was developing a mostly unexplainable interest in fly fishing. I had been reading about it, primarily in two books that someone had loaned to my father. One was The Trout Fisherman's Bible by Dan Holland. I can still recall and recite nearly verbatim the photo captions in this book.

One of them, beneath a photo of a huge brown trout from the Madison River, read, "Anyone can tell at a glance that this old boy was king of the pool." The other book, with even more powerful influence, was "Trout," by Ray Bergman. Published in 1938, it contained compelling and instructive writing with frequent references to Montana's Madison and Firehole Rivers, especially in a chapter titled "Experiences with the Dry Fly."

The alignment of these two things—reading about Montana and going there to fish—was how I initially came under the spell of Big Sky Country.

Later, likely in the pages of the "big three" magazines—Field & Stream, Outdoor Life, and Sports Afield—I became aware of the fishing and writing of fly-fishing's trail blazer, Joe Brooks. He appeared to be a slightly more contemporary writer who also extolled the virtues of Montana. I saw a photo of him displaying, as I recall, an eight-pound brown trout from the Yellowstone River, caught on a streamer, likely a Muddler Minnow.

In those years, and after, it seemed that everywhere I turned in the outdoor and fly-fishing press I saw Montana-this and Yellowstone Park-that stories. It appeared that if an outdoor magazine aimed to maximize newsstand sales, all it had to do was find a reason to put the word "Montana" somewhere on the cover.

Another significant book came to my attention several

years later, titled *Larger Trout for the Western Fly Fisherman*, by Charles E. Brooks, who resided—yes, you guessed it—near West Yellowstone, Montana. His writings in this and subsequent books, such as *The Trout and the Stream*, *The Living River*, a biography of the Madison, were focused on the area around Yellowstone Park.

Other writers were also jumping on the Montana bandwagon, including Ernest Schwiebert, who held the title of the "world's leading fly fisher," for a time, Dave Whitlock, Gary Borger, and others of influence and celebrity.

Even Montana's tackle stores were revered. Fly shops like Bud Lilly's and Pat Barnes' in West Yellowstone, and particularly Dan Bailey's in Livingston, were as famous as the trout streams nearby. To young impressionable fly fishers, it somehow felt important to get our tackle from these places: "You got a new rod? Where'd you get it?" "Dan Bailey's catalog."

Years later, when I finally visited Bailey's store, I did what every first-timer through that door did: I stared at the racks of rods, the walls of fly-tying material, and especially at the "Wall of Fame." On this wall, wooden outlines of one huge trout after another were displayed, many of them caught by my fly-fishing heroes such as Lee Wulff, Joe Brooks, Charles Waterman, Dave Whitlock, Gary Borger, and more and more. The realization that all these people had undoubtedly stood in this place and likewise gawked at this wall was inspiring. Towards the back of the shop, there was a room where the magic was created—rows of women fly tiers cranking out Royal Wulffs, Muddlers, and Spuddlers by the score. In more recent times, a beautiful wooden drift boat has reposed in the front of the store.

I don't think I was aware of it, but I was not the only impressionable person being swept into the seductive realm of Montana fly fishing. By the 1970s, Montana had taken firm hold throughout the North American fly-fishing culture and community. The cumulative effect was that we believed—because so many experts had said so—that the best fly fishing in North America, perhaps in the world, was in Montana.

So, this young Canadian kid, now completely obsessed by fly fishing, yearned to fish these rivers with these people's flies and methods, important and requisite steps in a pilgrimage of sorts, a rite of passage into the world of "real" fly fishing.

By the late 1960s, I had completed high school, was fresh into the freedom of a driver's license, and was finally able to do nearly as much fishing as reading about it. In October of 1970 I fished an Alberta river named the Bow, downstream of the soon-to-burgeon city of Calgary. In my early years on the river, the small number of fly fishers there fished mainly streamers and caught mainly rainbow trout, most of them between 16 and 22 inches long. I thought this was very good fishing, but as a Canadian I knew I had to be missing something. How could fishing be this good and not be in Montana?

A revelation occurred one day in the mid-1970s, when I was on a fly-fishing vacation to—yes—Montana. I went to get the genuine stuff you see, not the made-in-Alberta imitation. I was absorbing the atmosphere and essence of real fly fishing by hanging around in Bud Lilly's Trout Shop in West Yellowstone.

I waited patiently till the other customers were otherwise occupied and then nervously asked the man behind the counter—Bud himself—how the fishing had been recently. "Pretty good," he replied. "A fellow caught an 18-incher in the Madison two weeks ago." This answer struck me oddly. I thought, "An 18-incher two weeks ago? That's news? Here? In Montana? On the Madison River?" It hit me funny because I was pretty sure somebody would have caught an 18-incher back home on the Bow within the last hour.

I began guiding fly fishers on the Bow in about 1975. I got the job because I had fished the river some and had my summers off from the University of Alberta. We continued to fish mainly streamers, but one day, perhaps because it was a new occurrence or perhaps because I'd simply become more observant, I began to find these big fish feeding on the surface, eating mayflies that seemed to be pale morning duns. Later that season I saw another mayfly I'd recently read about in *Fly Fisherman* magazine. These were Trico-rythodes—"tricos" or "trikes" to the hep fly fishers—and the Bow's rainbows were eating them by the mouthful in gentle riffles each morning. There were also stifling hatches of caddisflies every evening near dark.

My appreciation for the quality of our fishing was confirmed further when I found myself guiding several of my heroes on the Bow. Those same fly-fishing writers who had convinced me of Montana's incontestable virtue, including Brooks, Borger, and Schwiebert, were now raving about an Alberta river. Perhaps it was then that I forsook my Canadian instinct to apologize for how good the fishing was on the Bow.

But here's the thing. The fishing I had and still have near home in Alberta is as good as that in most of Montana, but I still go to Montana to fish. People ask me why. They ask if it's better than Alberta. It's not a matter of better I tell them; it's a matter of different. For me, at least, it's a chance to step into the waters I read about as a kid, to experience again the streams that were formative to my fly-fishing education and passion.

Even now it sounds sacrilegious to say it, but the truth is that there is comparable and even better fishing in some places sometimes than that in Montana. But those places are not in Montana, and I guess that's my point. All aspects of North American fly fishing, from the aesthetics of the settings to the quality of the fish, to the bug hatches and the sport's significance to local culture, are unofficially measured against the "Montana Scale." Whether it has the best fly fishing or not doesn't matter anymore. For a fly angler today, there is still no other place with such mystique and attraction, and no other assemblage of syllables that carries the charisma, anticipation, and inexorable pull, as Mon-ta-na.

Jim McLennan was one of the first fly-fishing guides on Alberta's Bow River, and is a well-known outdoor writer and speaker. He is the author of five books on fly fishing, including his latest book, Trout Tracks. He is contributing editor for Fly Fisherman and Fly Fusion magazines. Jim is also co-host, along with Derek Bird, of Fly Fusion Television, a series broadcast on the World Fishing Network.

TWO

WAITING FOR IRIS

Kaitlyn Okrusch

Many of us have a deep and unexplainable relationship to the places we come from. At certain
moments home pulls us closer; at others it pushes us
away. This tension between push and pull felt real as I
packed up my belongings to leave my Montana home. I
was flying 2,500 miles east to attend graduate school in
New England. As I soared through the sky I wondered
what Iris was feeling at that moment. We were both starting journeys into the unknown that very August day, and
I found some comfort in that. It also helped knowing that
Iris and I always return to our Montana homes.

Iris is a river hawk, an osprey. She has summered in
Hellgate Canyon along the Clark Fork River near Missoula for about 25 years which makes her one of the oldest
documented living ospreys in the world. She has raised
each of her many offspring in the canyon and is a fierce

mother and survivor. She lives near the precise junction of great trout rivers Norman Maclean knew so well and is also known to be an excellent fisher. The unique speckling in her left eye accounts for her name. Every spring, people far and wide wait to see if she will return to her nest for yet another year.

Ospreys are commonly referred to as fish hawks, sea hawks, or river hawks. They are often confused with gull-like birds due to their angled wing silhouette, plumage coloring, and association with water. However, ospreys are raptors—specifically, hawks. Ospreys are birds of prey like other hawks, owls, eagles, and vultures. Their razor-sharp talons, forward-facing eyes, and pronounced hooked bills are adapted to hunt, kill, and eat meat. Most raptors eat smaller birds, rodents, reptiles, or carrion. Ospreys almost exclusively eat fish. They are one of six bird species found on every continent except for Antarctica, in part because they are excellent fishers and can eat both fresh and salt water fish. Where there are water and fish, there are probably ospreys.

Climate influences their migration patterns. In the north, due to freezing winter temperatures, lakes and rivers often become unfishable. Ospreys of the Canadian boreal forest and the northern U.S. migrate south every fall. The resident ospreys in Florida live relatively easier lives compared to the migratory birds of the north. Some migratory ospreys travel several thousand miles each year back and forth between their nesting and wintering grounds.

Ospreys tend to return to the same nest each breeding season. Returning to the same nest over and over again saves time and energy as their nests can weigh up to 300 lbs. Nesting in the same place each year means they also know their territory well. Life is more predictable when you know the rivers and streams, the mountains and valleys, and your neighbors and potential mates.

Like many other raptors, ospreys usually mate for life, although, Iris's circumstances are somewhat different. She has raised several chicks to adulthood with several mates over the years. We know all of this thanks to the dedicated work of the Montana Osprey Project which works in conjunction with Cornell Lab of Ornithology. They installed an osprey camera focused on Iris's nest so that we might better understand osprey behavior. Anyone can log on and peek into Iris's world from the time she arrives in March through early April. She normally leaves in late August. I know people who leave the webcam on their office computer screens so they can share time while she's in Montana. An entire Facebook group exists to share observations about her behavior. She is beloved.

I have been curious about ospreys since I was young. I remember seeing enormous clusters of twigs and branches stacked, twisted, and twirled into giant nests high on top of power line poles, trees, or other man-made platforms as my dad and I floated down the river. I remember large, magnificent brown and white birds—familiar by sight but unfamiliar by name—perched proudly on their stick kingdoms as we floated by. Seeing ospreys meant a day on the river fly fishing with my dad. We would listen to John Prine as he delivered mini natural history lessons. We would both learn from the river on those trips. I didn't realize then that those ospreys that so captured my attention might just be the greatest trout fishers of all—and that one day as a part of my work for the Clark Fork Watershed Education Program, I would study them so that I could teach others about these wonders of nature.

Four subspecies of Osprey exist. Birds from every subspecies plunge gracefully into the water to snag unsuspecting fish. They have long, slender legs and have wingspans of around 5-ft wide. Females are almost always about 20 percent larger than males. They have a distinct "M" shaped silhouette when in flight. Their wings have just enough surface area to allow hovering in the air so they can scan for fish near the water's surface. When diving, they carve through the air and can reach nearly 50 miles per hour on their descent.

Ospreys have the ability to move their fourth toe freely. This adaptation allows them to maneuver a fish in their talons so that the fish faces forward and is easier to fly back to nest to feed their young. The bottom of an osprey's feet are covered with what look like tiny spikes. These spicules feel like sandpaper and help an osprey hold onto slippery trout both underwater and in the air.

Ospreys catch fish that sometimes weigh as much as they do. They expend vast amounts of energy getting both themselves and the fish out of the water and sometimes drown due to exhaustion. The distinct curvature of an osprey's talons resembles the hooks fly tyers use for scud or caddis larvae patterns. Once an osprey rises out of the water with its catch, gravity, along with their unique talons, ensures the fish will make it back to the nest.

The keel is a bony extension of a bird's sternum or breastbone where the pectoral muscles attach. Ospreys have a much larger keel compared to other flying birds. This enlarged keel makes sense, considering the strength needed to catch and pull a fish out of the water that weighs nearly as much as the osprey itself.

Most raptors do not spend their days plunging fully into water to catch fish. Ospreys, like waterfowl, have developed a somewhat larger than normal preening gland. On birds, the preening gland sits at the base of the tail on the back and secretes an oily substance. Ospreys use their beaks to spread the oily mixture over each feather which makes them water resistant.

Ospreys have extremely dense feather barbs. If we examined a single osprey feather, we would see a complex matrix of structures. These barbs are like velcro. The barbs further branch out into millions of barbules, which are designed to stick to one another. This creates a smooth, cohesive shield making osprey feathers even more water resistant.

While all of these facts are interesting, I have found that the best way to learn about the osprey is to spend time watching one—for me it was Iris in Hellgate Canyon. Like the flow state one can enter while fly fishing, osprey observation suspends my sense of time and grounds me in the here and now. It also connects me with the birds I am studying in a way that is hard to put into words. My connection with Iris is deeper than just our moments together.

As a fifth-generation Montana woman, I am proud to come from the Upper Clark Fork River watershed near its headwaters in Butte. Butte's copper mining past is well-documented, as is mining's profound impact on the condition of the watershed's complex ecosystems. The EPA's National Priority List Superfund sites that interlock along the entire Upper Clark Fork River from Butte to Missoula form one of the nation's largest contiguous Superfund complexes. For many decades, the citizens of the headwater regions have been working and fighting to mitigate the grave ecological threats that continue to exist due to the region's mining past. While much progress has been made, especially upstream, the river will always will be precariously situated—one massive flood event from another environmental disaster. That's why we study Iris. She, like the river's

Iris lays the first egg of the season at Hellgate Osprey Nest, May 8, 2023.
Photo: Cornell Lab of Ornithology, Cornell University Bird Cam on the
University of Montana campus, Missoula, Montana.

citizens, continues to make a life in this hard-used water-shed. We can learn from her experience.

Ospreys are obligate carnivores—they exist at the top of the food chain. This means that they can be a direct indicator of a river ecosystem's condition. The aquatic plants and algae, the insects that feed on the plants and algae, and the fish that feed on those insects, become a direct conduit for the metals still present in the river, from fish to ospreys.

The Upper Clark Fork and Big Hole Rivers are both about 20 miles from Butte, separated by the Continental Divide. The Big Hole flows into the Jefferson, then into the Missouri, and eventually into the Mississippi before contributing its flow to the Gulf of Mexico. The Clark Fork of the Columbia eventually makes its way to the Pacific Ocean.

Growing up in Butte allowed me to split time in both watersheds. I was able to explore each one and note their often-marked differences. The Big Hole ecosystem has its own challenges, but has remained relatively pristine when compared to the Upper Clark Fork. But, as a kid, I remember seeing ospreys along both rivers. It is the same now, with populations of ospreys thriving on both the Big Hole and the Clark Fork. In spite of the obvious differences between these rivers, it is a hopeful sign that fish hawks can survive on both.

As a Montana woman and an admirer of birds, I take Iris the Osprey as an example of inspiration and strength. She is my muse. I am thankful that we are connected together through our home watershed. Like Iris, even though I left home, I am called to return someday.

Every year that Iris returns is a year of celebration. She has allowed us to deepen our own knowledge and connection to our freshwater ecosystems. Iris was last seen on her nest on August 20, 2022—the exact date I flew from Montana to New England. I can only hope that her strong wings and wild spirit carry her home, safely, once again. Until then, I will be watching the webcam and waiting for Iris.

Editor's note: Iris returned this year to her nest in Hellgate Canyon on April 8, 2023.

⌒

Kaitlyn Okrusch holds a M.S. in Environmental Studies and currently teaches middle school science. She has worked on various bird projects over the past decade conducting research, developing curriculum, and educating the public. Her passion is fueled by connecting people with the wild spaces they call home—especially through birds.

THREE

AS GOOD AS GOLD

Pat Munday

I'M AN historian and a philosopher, and bring these perspectives to my love of trout fishing and the places where trout live. I was fortunate to grow up in a trout fishing paradise with family and friends who were avid anglers, and equally fortunate to move to southwest Montana where, as author Norman Maclean said, there is no clear line between religion and fly fishing. I was also fortunate to arrive in Butte in 1990, just as Superfund clean-up and restoration were getting underway, and to play a small but active role in that process. Through my involvement in Superfund, I came to realize that in this postmodern world we cannot take trout and clean water for granted. Along the way, I had many river teachers from both the human and natural worlds.

From love stems obligation. I developed a love for fishing at a young age. Gradually this love extended to the places that fish—especially trout—lived. As I grew into adulthood, I realized that the gift of love does not come free. Quality fishing—that is, fish from natural, sustainable populations and good habitat—comes about because anglers and other environmentally minded folks demand good government management of our land and water resources. My life has been shaped by fishing, the places where I fished, and the people who I fished with. Moreover, I have invested countless hours working with public and government groups to ensure that future generations might also benefit from quality fishing.

In the beginning, it was like a cartoon about fishing. Grandma bent a small brass safety pin into a hook, Gramps cut a finger-thick willow to serve as a rod, and Uncle Jim found a length of string in his glovebox. There were no rocks to be turned over for worms at Presque Isle State Park, so a piece of wiener became the bait. I could see bluegills swarming in the shallows of the pond near the pavilion that held our family reunion. It was summer, in a few weeks I would turn four years old, and I caught my first fish. I still remember screaming in surprise as the bluegill's dorsal fin spines pierced my tender palm. No one paid much attention to a child's pain in the 1950s, but Uncle Jim did cut the top off a milk carton so I could bring the fish home. Grandma cleaned and cooked it for me the next morning, and because Uncle Jim had told me the fish's belly was orange because it had an egg inside, I was convinced that the fried egg—sunny side up—Grandma served me with the bluegill came from the fish.

That's how it began. Fishing has been an important part of my life since that time, beginning with sunfish and horned dace and, by age eight, graduating to trout. Gramps and his friend, Bernard Dutka, had a good sense of priorities. Once or more each week from spring through summer, they would close up Bernie's truck repair shop early for a late afternoon/evening of trout fishing. Happily, closing time usually coincided with the end of my school day. Later, as a teenager, I sometimes skipped school with friends and we would hitchhike to and from a nearby trout stream. In junior high school, my friend Jeff Armstrong and I joked about how important it was to break up with your girlfriend in early April before the opening of trout season. By high school, I learned to date only girls who had the patience for fishing and a tolerance for mosquitoes.

I grew up on the headwaters of the Allegheny River in Pennsylvania, near the New York State border. Tunungwant Creek, which flowed through my little city of Bradford, was heavily polluted with sewage, seepage from abandoned oil wells, and oil refinery waste. Not a good place to fish. Within a 30-minute drive, however, lay many excellent trout streams. Early on, fishing with Gramps and Bernie, I bonded with the waters of Sugar Run and Kinzua Creek. Small, freestone streams with base flows of 10 to 20 cubic feet per second, fishing them was an intimate experience. With a mile or two of walking, I found solitude in reaches with robust populations of wild, self-sustaining brown and native brook trout in addition to the usual put-and-take hatchery fish.

Gramps and Bernie generally used flyrods but typically baited with worms, salmon eggs, or salted minnows. They fly fished occasionally with streamers or bucktails, but it was my older cousin "Uncle" Don Bradish who schooled me on fly fishing. Uncle Don was a professional engineer with a career in California, but each summer he came home to visit the creeks of his youth. He regaled me with stories of fishing in Yellowstone Park and other exotic locations, and on his visits, we fished Kinzua Creek for its sometimes-sizable brown trout. It was a July morning, the summer I turned fourteen. Kinzua Creek was in low summer flow, and my go-to bait choice of garden worms was not producing. Stalking through the creek-side brush, I watched Uncle Don cast a White Miller to a large boulder in my favorite pool. He set up on a heavy fish and soon brought to net a brown trout of elbow-to-fingertip length. I sauntered over as he gently released the fish and gave me a warm smile. I was hooked. Each summer until my high school graduation I benefited from a lesson as well as a pocketful of traditional dry and wet flies. I cherished the magic held by each tiny Adams, Royal Wulff, or Parmachene Belle and in the winter months, I dreamed of the trout that I would catch come spring.

As a boy I didn't usually wear a hat and Uncle Don saw this as a problem. Perhaps it was because I once interrupted my cast to brush mosquitoes away from my face and inadvertently dropped my line across his shoulders. Not that I was a great caster and even my best efforts were limited by the cheap level line on my reel. At any rate, as we left his car the next morning he pulled a spare hat out of his gear bag and handed it to me. "It'll keep the skeeters out of your eyes."

I'm not sure it did, but somehow it, made me feel more like a fly fisherman. A real fly fisherman. Somebody who could wade into Yellowstone waters and catch big cutthroat trout until his arms got tired. Somebody who knew the difference between a Red Fox Squirrel Nymph and a Gold-Ribbed Hare's Ear. Wearing the hat, I could feel some of Uncle Don's character seep into my head. The hat changed who I was, or at least who I thought I was, which is probably the same thing, or so my behavioral therapist wife tells me. Over the years I became a great believer in this variation of "the clothes make the man" theory. Carrying my grandfather's Case XX jackknife, hunting whitetail deer with a friend's flintlock rifle, wearing a hand-me-down Woolrich buffalo plaid jacket from an older cousin—through each of these things and countless others it seems I acquired new personas. Not the shallow Jungian masks of mere conformation, but deep patterns that became part of my own archetypal identity.

∐

I moved to Montana in 1990 for a faculty job with a small college in Butte. I interviewed in March and it didn't hurt that my host and prospective department head, Tommy Lester, and I drank the better part of a case of beer and talked until 3 a.m. The next day, after a late breakfast, we fished the Jefferson River. It was a warm spring day and I caught an 18-inch rainbow that leapt from the water like nothing I had ever experienced on Eastern trout streams. There was no mention of a fishing license.

My wife, infant daughter, and I settled into Butte. I spent that August and September scouting the local mountains for trout fishing and elk hunting spots. Raised on the small streams of north-central Pennsylvania, I found the Jefferson and Big Hole Rivers overwhelming. Instead, I sought out small streams. Silver Bow Creek flows northward from Butte to form the Clark Fork River, but it was clearly not an option. The riparian zone was a moonscape after a century of copper mining and smelting had made Butte ground zero for America's largest Superfund site. Silver Bow Creek was the river that ran through it, Butte style.

German Gulch Creek, a major tributary of Silver Bow Creek, was a different story. From the late nineteenth through the early twentieth century it had been a mecca for gold placer mining, but that sort of wealth was long gone. Prospecting the creek where it ran along a Forest Service road, I dappled a fly in a spot of pocket water and was rewarded with a fat, sassy Eastern brook trout. In Pennsylvania, our native brook trout were special treasures found in only a few small headwater streams. In Montana, however, I learned they were an exotic and invasive pest, with the limit set at twenty fish or ten pounds per day, whichever came first. I never caught the ten-pound limit, but many days I brought home a basket of twenty fish.

In German Gulch, I discovered modern-day gold and the Montana equivalent of brook trout: westslope cutthroat trout. Descended from a common ancestor of rainbow trout, westslopes (also known as cutties) diverged from other cutthroat species in the past few million years—an era coinciding with the ebb and flow of glaciers during the Pleistocene. Shaped by short summer growth seasons, low water nutrient levels, and high stream gradients, cutties seldom pass up a meal. Unlike their wary brown trout cousins, cutties will hang out in fast shallow water on a sunny day and eat every bug or minnow within reach. This makes for a remarkably catchable fish, a virtue fly anglers appreciate. Drift a fly over a brown trout and, if the fly closely matches insects on the water, it might have a look. Cutties, on the other hand, are not selective. They're on a seefood diet, you know, "see food, eat food".

Without angling restrictions, cutties are too catchable for their own good. In the late nineteenth century, as ranching and mining and other forms of industrial economic development came to Montana, market hunting and fishing were the order of the day. On the nearby Big Hole River, for example, commercial fishermen collected great quantities of native Arctic grayling and cutties, salted them in barrels, and shipped them to Butte and other mining settlements.

By the 1880s, Montana's native fisheries were seriously depleted. Fish weirs, dynamite, and other commercial means of taking fish were outlawed, but sport anglers now wanted to catch fish. Montana and the federal government built hatcheries as did private groups and individuals such as Butte's copper king, William A. Clark. The era of indiscriminate stocking began with species including Eastern brook trout, California rainbow trout, and German brown trout. Gradually, these fish took hold as wild, self-sustaining populations. Few cared about cutties or other native fish.

My life coincided with the environmental movement. Beginning with Rachel Carson's book *Silent Spring* (1962) and culminating with federal legislation such as the *Clean Water Act* (1972) and the *Comprehensive Environmental Response, Compensation and Liability Act* (1980; aka Superfund Law), America was determined to make up for a century of neglect when it came to natural resource management.

History matters. Buttians know the cost of environmental damages and the meaning of "protection" in

Environmental Protection Agency. In grade school, my daughter had her finger pricked to determine whether she had lead in her blood. Folks from the local EPA office visited our home to test for toxic dust in the walls and metals in the yard soil. In 1983, Silver Bow Creek had been declared a Federal Superfund site with the listing expanded to include Butte in 1987. As a historian of technology and the environment, and as an avid angler, I became intensely interested in and heavily involved with various grassroots groups that helped guide remedy and restoration in the upper Clark Fork River watershed.

Silver Bow Creek and its German Gulch tributary were a great restoration success story and by 2010, westslope cutthroat trout recolonized a watershed where they had been poisoned off for more than a century. Many anglers don't care about native fish in their original habitat. So long as they're catching fish, they call it good. Fly fishing people, on the other hand, do care. Most of us, anyway. Are we elitist snobs? Well, that too. But the burden of knowledge also plays a role. It's like the old joke repeated by Norman Maclean's father, a Presbyterian preacher: "A Methodist is just a Baptist who can read." I guess fly fishing people are anglers who can read. And once you know about biogeography and the evolution of the fourteen or so subspecies of cutthroat trout in ecological niches across the West, it's hard to accept their replacement by invasive Eastern brook trout. Or maybe it's the tyranny of knowledge as we become trapped in what we think we know. At some point, it's time to leave the philosophy behind, tie on a size 14 Royal Wulff, and catch some fish.

It's late afternoon on an early August day. The steep walls of Durant Canyon shade Silver Bow Creek and though it's a hot day, my feet ache with cold as I wet wade my way up the stream. Below the confluence with German Gulch Creek the water forms excellent pockets as it wears its way through lava flows that must have blocked the stream twenty million years ago. I've taken a few big cutties from this reach and it's exciting to catch eighteen-inch fish from a creek that my Lab can almost leap across. My feet are cold though, so I climb up the south-facing slope high enough to sit in the sun for a bit. In a pretty little pipe I carved from wood sawn from the crotch of an apple tree years ago, I burn a bowl of pot. I'm stoned and starting to appreciate the break from fishing.

As blood circulation returns to my feet, I notice the wild nodding onions growing on the hillside meadow. I've killed two brook trout for supper, they're nestled in a sheaf of wet grass in my creel. Wild onions, like the ramps we dug in the Alleghenies, are delicious with trout. As the French *terroir* expression goes, "things that grow together go together." I set to digging a handful of bulbs. Thinking of sliced onions stuffed into the bellies of foil-wrapped trout on the grill, the mere act of digging the little onions makes me salivate.

Thunder booms along the valley walls and I look up to see a thunderstorm blowing in. I hurriedly rub dirt from the last onion, drop it into my basket, and start downstream to my old Land Rover which is nearly two miles away. Within ten minutes I'm soaking wet and shivering with cold as the temperature drops twenty degrees and the wind rises. Crossing a watering access point where a fenced path allows the local rancher's cattle to drink at the creek, I see brown fabric flapping in the wind. Some ranch hand has left his Carhartt vest hanging on a fence post. I put it on, zip it up, and think myself very lucky to find this fine warm thing.

I haven't walked two hundred yards when an eerie feeling creeps over me. It's not the happy feeling of wearing Uncle Don's fishing hat or the comfort of Gramps' knife snug in the pocket of my jeans. Dark feelings seep into me like the rain soaking through my clothes. Who was this ranch hand and what was he so angry about? I feel his quiet rage at the incessant task of mending fences, dealing with ornery mama cows, and abiding a high-handed ranch owner who pays his hands half of what they're worth. It could be the delirium of hypothermia making me feel this way, or just some paranoid side road from the pot I smoked. The dark feelings grow with each step and I'm increasingly convinced that the vest is seriously bad karma. The Rover is in sight now, on the abandoned railroad grade and just a half-mile away. I shuck the vest and hang it on a low limb of a Douglas fir tree. By the time I reach the Rover I'm warmed up and feeling better, although it pains me that I neglected to stop and pick up the two beers I left to chill in a shallow side eddy of the creek. Oh well, my gift to the next passing angler. No ill feelings could possibly haunt a bottle of beer.

I'm an old man now. Like the seasons, everything turns in circles though some circles are bigger than other circles. I fish the same creeks and rivers each spring and summer with no desire to catch salmon in Alaska or brown trout in Patagonia. A light rain jacket lives in the rear pouch of my fishing vest so I'm not tempted to wear clothing found hanging on fence posts. German Gulch Creek and Silver Bow Creek and Kinzua Creek were my Wisdom

Rivers, teaching me the importance of remedy and restoration for our natural world as well as for our own souls. Environmentally, we can restore what was and maintain what is. Personally, I have returned to the simple wonder of my four-year old self, happy to catch wild native fish on a willow rod and bent pin.

Pat Munday is an environmentalist, writer, and college professor living in Butte, Montana. He is the author of Montana's Last Best River: The Big Hole and its People. *(Lyons Press, 2001) and was awarded the Liebig-Woehler Freundschaft Prize for scholarship in the history of chemistry, and contributions through environmental activism.*

WISDOM RIVER

FOUR

POEMS AND MUSINGS

Doris Daley

Al (Doc) Mehl

Larry Kapustka

Chad Okrusch

WILLOW CREEK

Doris Daley

You'd think a prairie girl's memories would
    scratch like wheat chaff.
smell like hay,
howl like a Chinook wind blasting off the
    mountains
and taste like wild saskatoons picked on a hot
    July day.
And you'd be right.

Yet my first memories float up from the little
    creek that ran below the house.

I lost my glasses in that creek and—a
    miracle!—found them two days later in
    the mud below the stepping stones.
I saw my dad, wearing nothing more than
    his underwear and a cowboy hat, wade
    through chest-deep pools to rescue a calf
    stranded by a flood.

We built rafts out of rotted fence posts and
    baler twine, sailed to magical coves rife with
    pirates, and were home in time for supper.
Beaver, deer, kids, minnows and frogs lived a
    rich aquatic life in that ancient, meandering
    creek.

The farm house, the color of buffalo beans, is
    gone now. Sold for scrap.
No school bus comes down the road anymore.
    No kids.
The old granary burned down in the '96 fire.
The hay field is rented out now; nobody can
    afford the machinery.

Only the creek is still there. Will always be there.
Or will it? The new owners want to subdivide.

THE MOTHER

Al (Doc) Mehl

If you have seen the river,
  Then you have seen the Mother.

If you have seen the rainbow,
  Spanning the gorge,
  Spanning the ages,
  Casting the refracted rays of an unseen sun,
  Then you have seen the Mother.

If you have seen the sky afire,
  Peach-red glow over the black mountain
  embers,
Fanned by the desert winds, not yet aflame
But ready to burst impending inferno,
Then you have known the Mother.

If you the seen the sacred datura,
  Waved away the insistent sphinx moth in
  dusk's low light,

And smelled the musty invitation of the
unfolding petals,
Gazed upon the lily-white bloom that has
burst upon the early night
As if to steal the thunder from the moon,
Then you have stood beside the Mother.

If you have known the mole,
    If you have known the turtle,
    If you have tasted of the fertile harvest,
    Then you have walked with the Mother.

If you have seen the river,
    If you have met the river,
    If you have known the river,

Then you have known the Mother.

WATER

Al (Doc) Mehl

Living in my city is like living in a lie,
Because we try to alter nature, and make wet what should
     be dry.
This land was prairie pasture, and the grass was thin, but
     long.
We replaced it with a carpet turf, and groomed it for a lawn.

And as it grows, we clip it short, those blades of green and
     blue,
Plant flowers 'round the border and young trees around it
     too.
For greener lawns, we fertilize, and then, in years we're
     lucky,
We water it with gallons, and pretend we're in Kentucky.

We use the water freely, inside the house and out,
And we only slow our use a bit when they announce, "It's
     drought!"
Old timers, they will tell you that this drought is no
     surprise,
But we use the water freely, as the reservoirs go dry.

We use the water freely, just ignoring what's in store,
Because when the water's running low, we'll buy ourselves
    some more!
We buy it from the farmers and the ranchers to the east.
And when nobody's selling, we all know it can be leased.

They're selling back those water rights acquired through
    the years.
And though they'll take the money, they're all fighting back
    the tears,
Because they've sold off all the cattle, and they've boarded
    up their homes.
The only cowboys left out there are writing cowboy poems.

The cows have disappeared. There's no more grain to
    make the bread.
There's no more corn to serve beside it, and the berries,
    they're all dead,
Because the corn rows never flowered, and the wheat is
    only chaff.
There's no water left for crying. Only crows hang 'round to
    laugh.

But us city folk, we're looking fine. Our lawns are turning
    green,
And the plants are showing flowers just as pretty as you've
    seen.
If you ask us how we're doing, well, we're in a fickle mood.
We're now swimming in the water! But we sure could use
    some food.

OPEN AND SHUT

Doris Daley

Old Man. Piikani. Kainai.
Pekisko. Livingstone. Waldron. Crowsnest.
English, Blackfoot...these names taste sweet on the
    tongue. They are
Names as familiar and as timeless
As a trout rising for a mayfly, a grizzly routing for ants.
Now what? Are we to replace them with words like
Damage assessment? Selenium leaching? Policy gaps?
    Benga Mining?
Seems like a bad trade: rivers and hills millions of years
    in the making for a
Hell-bound train full of coal. Somewhere north of the
    Crowsnest,
Under a Chinook Arch, the Trickster is waiting.
Think about that.

BOSS OF MOUNTAIN WATER

Larry Kapustka

Mountain streams tumble through rapids and pools.
Here the turbulent water picks up oxygen and is cold.
If you are lucky, you may see the iridescent flash
of a massive bull trout consuming her prey voraciously.
Lucky, because this boss is elusive
as she navigates the waters showing her inherent power.

Gravel and sizeable river stones are rounded by the
    water's power
as it plunges over and between rock slabs into pools.
Survival amidst pummelling quartz shrapnel requires
    being elusive.
Nature can be indiscriminately cold.
Inhabiting such hostile environs demands cunning as
    appetites are voracious.
Vigilance is needed to capture tantalizing food items that
    zip by in a flash.

When the light is just right, a quick arching lunge creates
    a brilliant flash.
Water crashing downward at speed of attacking osprey
    has great power.
Grabbing prey at that speed requires a keen attitude to
    serve the voraciousness.

Survival is a challenge in tumbling rapids and shallow
    pools.
Even in late summer, snowmelt supplying the stream
    is cold.
Any creature surviving here must be fit and elusive.

The bull trout's large size is a testament to its
    elusiveness.
As a juvenile she could become prey to any predator in
    a flash.
Her growth is slow as its metabolism is constrained by
    the cold.
Yet, she must be aggressive in the narrow window of
    mountain summers to gain power.
To avoid predation from eagles and bears, she inhabits
    turbulent rapids and deep pools.
That she achieves lunker size attests to her cunning
    and voraciousness.

When she attacks a trout or mountain whitefish, she is
    voracious.
Prior to the strike, the aggressor is elusive.
She darts out of the confines of log jams that frame
    pools
to capture a meal in a flash,
then quickly retreats to the depths of the plunge pool
    conserving power.
Imposing human ethos to the scene, one might judge
    the predation as cold.

Spawning occurs in early fall and fertilized eggs
    develop during winter's cold.
In the last days before ice-up, young and old consume
    all types of prey voraciously,
preparing for the long period of torpor to maximize
    their springtime power.

With summer waters waning, the bull trout must
     become even more elusive.
In the warm shallow waters, her life can be
     extinguished in a flash.
so, she seeks the cool oxygenated water that rapids
     feed into pools.

Amidst the waters cold
     swims a monster trout so elusive.
Her appetite for fish, crustaceans, and insects is
     voracious;
     she darts from shadowy cover in a flash.
Her torpedo sleek body is built for power,
     letting her glide gracefully through rapids and
     pools.

*Editor's Note: A sestina is a poetic form that consists of six
lines per stanza and six stanzas; the last word of each line
rotates through in a pattern such that each ending work
occupies all six positions. In this variation, the poem ends
with a tercet in which there are three couplets using the
six end words.*

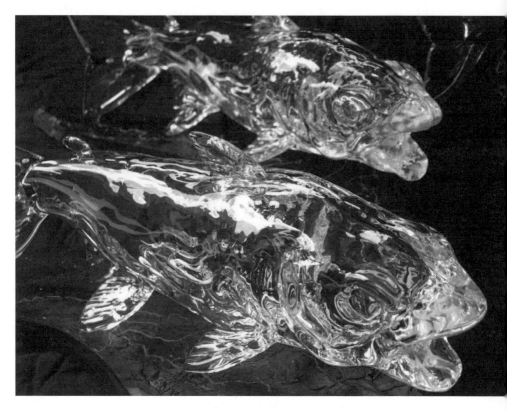

Bull Trout
Glass and Slate.
Artist: Tyler Rock
Firebrand Glass Studio, Diamond Valley, Alberta

MEDITATION ON FRESH WATER, ETHICS & BULL TROUT

Chad Okrusch

fresh water, bull trout
cold, clear, complex, connected
both precious and rare

WHEN ED ABBEY said we needed more predators, he wasn't talking about bull trout. He was talking about charismatic megafauna—grizzlies, wolves, cougars, and such. But I like to think that if Abbey had ever watched a 30-inch bull trout devour a wounded spring run Chinook salmon, or a runt-gosling, he'd have included this voracious predator on his list of species we need more of.

By 1999, bull trout made a different list: the list of threatened and endangered species. In Montana in the Flathead basin, biologists counted 1,152 bull trout in 1982. By 2023 this population had declined to 493. In Alberta, despite the fact that the bull trout is the provincial fish emblem, they are classified as "Threatened" under the *Wildlife Act*. Suffice to say that throughout their entire native range—roughly, the ecoregion we call the Pacific Northwest and parts of Western Canada—bull trout are on the brink.

We simply do not value them as we do other species.

In terms of aesthetics, many fish are more handsome than the big-headed bull trout. They were not blessed with visual beauty like rainbow or Yellowstone cutthroat.

Bull trout are of no use to us in terms of economics. They mature slowly, live long, maintain small predator-sized populations, and require complex habitat. In short, humans have little regard for bull trout because they can't be mass produced in the machinery of industrial hatcheries.

Many anglers trained in utility still consider bull trout a trash fish because they are piscivores—they eat other, valuable fish—like exotic summer runs of salmon.

Once upon a time, fishing guides on Oregon's McKenzie River caught and killed bull trout—for the good of the river. They hung them from bridges and barbed wire fences—like coyotes—and encouraged others to do the same.

But bull trout have value beyond human notions of aesthetics, economics, or utility. They have what Aldo Leopold called intrinsic value—value in-and-of-themselves. They have value just because they are.

Ecology has provided us yet another way to value bull trout—as an indicator of a robust system. Among all salmonids, bull trout may require the most pristine environment. Those who know refer to the bull trout's habitat needs refer to them as the 4Cs: cold, clear, complex, and connected.

Bull trout are thermally sensitive and live in streams that run clear and cold. They require complex habitat—lots of cover, large woody debris, boulders, undercut banks, and gravel spawning beds. They need riffles, runs, and pools. And, in order to continue existing, bull trout populations must be connected. Sadly, most are not.

One ten-thousandth of all water on Earth moves over land as rivers. Of all the river systems in the world, few are cold, clear, complex, and connected enough to support populations of wild bull trout. Even fewer exist in the bull trout's native range. We ought to value these places and these fish for no other reason than they continue to exist—in spite of us.

Rivers sustain us—humans and bull trout— regardless of how beautiful we are, or how much we contribute to the economy, or how useful we may be. In the grand scheme of things, our value is derived not from these factors, but from our very existence and from the sacred roles we play in natural systems.

◦∾

FIVE

THE VEIL

Kayla Lappin

A FLASH OF RAINBOW shot out across the reflection of the water as Kate knelt to reel in her catch. The strong trout struggled against the tension of the line.

"Don't worry buddy, I'm not keeping you." Its eyes met with Kate's, if only for a moment to say, "please," and Kate gently removed the hook out of the lip of the trout and gently set its body in the shallow of the river so it could swim free once again.

The last breath of summer murmured through the cottonwood trees that lined the smooth lull of the Jefferson River. Bursts of yellow and orange dotted the bottomland and the air was turning cooler. Fishing during the evening brought a glow of purple curtains on the Tobacco Root Mountains near Twin Bridges, and the first visitations of stars, especially at this hole, which her family called "The Jungle." Being here allowed Kate to set her thoughts straight with the world.

As she looked out at the crystalline surface, her heart glanced back at a time in her life when things felt simpler. If she listened closely enough, she would recall that little girl dressed up in an oversized sweatshirt, throwing rocks from the banks or turning over stones to look for stoneflies that would dart out and into the open water.

She could hear the sloshing of her grandfather's rubber waders in the stream as he came in from his last cast. Kate closed her eyes for a moment to bring herself into a memory that hung like pins in her chest. In the vision, her brother was about ten and she and her little sister were no more than seven. The worm castle they had made in the mud smelled of the algae that bloomed in late summer. The plastic Little Hugs drinks were covered in muddy hand prints as she and her sister explored the vastness of the riverbed.

Grandpa loved to be in the 'in between' place as he called it—the time after the sun fell behind the mountains, before the warm summer day gave way to the coolness of the river at night. Evenings in the 'in between', he'd take Kate, her sister Mary and the other grandkids over to the garage to select tools for adventure: dusty flies in boxes, the cheapest fly poles one could buy, and the reassuring feel of the coolers, packed with snacks. They'd all load up in the old Toyota Tacoma and sit on the tailgate as grandpa slowly crawled the truck over to the riverbed, a half mile away. Then came the approach of the Jungle, a thick place you couldn't drive through, and they'd hike through, looking over their backs for mountain lions that weren't actually there, or maybe a wolverine, like that one grandpa said he saw that one time.

"Wolverines are fierce and can attack at any moment," grandpa had said. The thrill of the wildlife and the pull of the water always meant time for exploring and finding one's place. It was an unspoken rule that you didn't bother grandpa once he was in the water. You could ask him for anything until that moment that his fishing vest was on and the fly rod went behind his back. You also didn't throw rocks in while he was fishing; unless you wanted his voice to boom out over the melody of the rushing water ... or over the rapids either. Don't disrupt the song, don't disrupt the dance.

In this time of quiet and exploration as a kid, Kate began to rely upon the cooler evenings and the slowness as a way to come to understand life. There were few things in life that couldn't be worked out over an hour's worth of evening fishing', she came to understand. And 'fishing', she came to understand, was less about catching than it was about being present to the gift of the moment. The water rushing, the coolness of the water from the confluence of the Big Hole just a few miles upstream. All beating together. All one.

Her throat began to swell at the memories and soft tears flowed down her cheeks.

"I miss him too." Her dad's footsteps made their way behind her. She had lost track of time for a moment. Kate's entire chest felt stretched and heavy. Maybe it was the feel of the change of the seasons, or the Sunday pre-work week blues, or catching a rainbow trout that had to be thrown back, but it seemed Kate could feel the weight of everything in her life building up on her.

"When does this heaviness go away?" Kate burst out. "It's been eight years. Eight years and I feel as lost as I did at 19 when he died. I'm not making a difference with any-thing. What am I doing with my life, marketing? Marketing is a joke. This whole thing is a joke." She looked up at her dad.

He looked at her while she sobbed. "Come here," he said, and he stretched out his arms. "Earning a living at a job is nothing to be ashamed about. You have a kid, now, that changes things too."

Kate remembered her breath and she inhaled sharply, the 'in between' time at the river was over. "Crap, we'd better get back to the house so I can nurse Lyla." She began to quickly pack up the fishing supplies.

Across the river, a bald eagle circled around and landed softly at the top of a cottonwood tree.

"Look!" her dad whispered excitedly as he pointed at the bird.

Kate looked across the water and up at the swaying cottonwood branches to the talons of a sovereign eagle. Something in Kate paused. And for a moment the eagle's eyes seemed to pierce right through her.

She brought her attention back to the fishing gear which she began to strap onto the front cargo hold of their four-wheeler. "Oh, cool! Gah, Dad, we'd better get back to Lyla." She said, anxiously.

On the way back to the house, as the sun made its final decent and the sky began to twinkle, Kate's mind didn't want to leave the in-between. She heard faintly in her head in her own voice, "What about being graceful with yourself, what about being okay to be right here?"

The pain in her chest lessened as the words sank into her body. The words 'graceful' and 'divine' hung in her mind as she made her way back to the house.

Monday morning arrived and Kate lay nervously awake in bed. Mondays felt like she had to hit the ground running. She rolled over in bed, nursed Lyla back to sleep and then as softly and quietly as possible, glided out of bed—not daring to breathe too loudly or move the blanket and wake the 11-month old.

She quickly put on her clothes, which she had set out the night before, grabbed her work bag, and tip-toed out of the room. She began to get bags ready for the day, which always seemed like endless juggle of work and life balance. Each time she washed the parts of her breast pump she felt a ping inside of herself. The guilt of leaving her child in someone else's care ate at her like ants picking over roadkill, gnawing, desperate, ravenous.

Giving birth had propelled Kate into a deep questioning of life, never before communicated to her, a side effect of bringing a soul into the world.

Kate's job didn't offer paid maternity leave, and when Lyla was 9-weeks old she left the familiar rhythm of Kate's ever-present heartbeat for the first time. The separation that formed that day grew inside of Kate's heart like a large fissure in a volcano.

After a while, Lyla woke up and Kate sat down to nurse her before her mom came to watch her for the day. Kate stroked her face as she rocked her in her grandmother's old rocking chair, singing:

> *Someday*
> *I'll be home,*
> *Someday,*
> *you'll know,*
> *Someday,*
> *I won't have to go,*
> *Someday,*
> *I'll get to hold you*
> *all day long.*

As she sang, the inside of Kate's chest stretched and pulled. Much like dangling on the end of a rope over a wide canyon, the bottom of the canyon far below. Guilt shook her all the way down to her feet.

What could be more important than staying home with Lyla during her first years of life? Why hadn't she prepared for this before she had kids? As much as she wanted to, she just couldn't seem to find purpose in her work. She felt like she was in the in-between with her life's purpose.

The sound of tires pulling up in the driveway alerted Kate that her mom, Kristen, was here to watch Lyla for the day. Kate kissed the top of Lyla's head and opened the front door for her mom. Kristen paused for a moment and brushed Kate's hair out of her face, saying, "The mornings do get better, Kate."

"I know, I know." Kate began to rush to grab her bags, wiping tears from her eyes.

"There's much to be said for a mom who provides for her children," Kristen called after Kate, who was busy grabbing bags and her car keys.

"Yeah, but, I bet those moms are doing what they are supposed to be doing with their lives!" Kate fired back, feeling anger rise within herself.

"I don't know about that," Kristen said back, taking Lyla into the kitchen.

Kate's eyes welled up and a lump grew in her throat, but she stuffed it back down. "Love you so much! See you later," Kate called as she left for work.

Kate turned on the radio and The Eagles' song, "Life in the Fast Lane," was playing on her stereo. Before she shut it off, she realized, there he was, The eagle from the river. But maybe that was just a coincidence.

As Kate made her way into her office and sat down at her desk, she opened her gratitude and dream journal and began to write out ten things she was grateful for, and ten dreams she wanted to manifest in her life. The practice helped her feel like she was moving somewhere, and in her busy mom life, ten minutes was all she could manage.

As she finished writing down her dreams for her life, her coworker, Adler, quietly walked into their shared office. Kate, whose desk was right by the door, looked up and said, "Hey Adler! How was your weekend?"

Adler replied as she walked past Kate to her desk, "Good! We didn't do much. How was yours?"

Kate replied, "Went fishing with my dad out in Silver Star, it was beautiful."

"Oh, nice!" Adler said as she sat behind her desk.

A big fundraiser for the non-profit she worked at was coming up soon. Kate was going over her to-do list for the planning. She rolled her chair out from her desk to check with Adler about a donation from her friend's clothing company.

"Hey did Kory come through with those..." Kate's voice trailed off.

Her mind began to fix on a vision of someone holding an older man's hands. The hands were wrinkled with deep veins with remarkably dark age spots. The hands were frail. Kate felt like the person they belonged to didn't have much time left in the world.

"Oh yeah, I asked Kory last week and he said I can stop by tomorrow and pick up the gift basket, he's also throwing in some coffee mugs." Alder responded from her desk.

"Coffee mugs?" Kate rolled her office chair out into the centre of the room so she could see Adler's desk.

"Yeah." Adler looked up.

Kate stared blankly at Adler.

"For the fundraiser…" Adler answered.

"Right, yes, perfect! That will go well in the auction." Kate said as she rolled her chair back to her desk.

Kate's phone lit up on her desk, with a text from her sister, Mary.

"Buckets." It read.

Kate responded: "Did you hear back from that job application?"

Mary replied: "Nope. It's been three weeks; I don't think I'm getting it."

"Well, just keep at it, you are going to find something." Kate texted back.

Mary sends: "Ahh, thanks. Just hard, I've been trying for months to get a job, and it's getting really hard to have faith right now."

Kate went to respond, but paused. She could feel Mary's heart racing even though she was hundreds of miles away. If only Mary could see what the rest of us see in her, Kate thought. Then words begin to pour out of Kate's fingers and into a text message like water:

As you move forward into the light and the purpose of your life, the details of life begin to swirl around you. All is felt, all is coming. You are at the dawn, the time before the birds wake up, the time before the stoneflies hatch. Look into your heart and trust that all is coming. Let go of the pain of the unknown and embrace the change that swirls all around. You are not lost; you are not broken. The time has come to see yourself as the one who is moving things forward. You cannot move into the place of security until the water has poured over your hands and spilled from your soul, all must be felt in order to move forward. All must be allowed to shine forth. Let go of the timing and trust in the journey, you are being taken care of.

Kate continued with a new text,

You must take care to listen to the call within, you must take care to carry the torch of the flame of your heart forward. The tenderness in your heart must be tended, opened, and poured outward. For within you stirs the call. Within you stirs the next steps. Allow yourself to let go, allow yourself to be free. You are making your dream happen, you must trust that with each attempt that passes, you are being brought forward to a place of truth, and a place of harmony with your soul. For as you move forward, you also bring forward your goals and dreams. Do not dwell on the steps, but rather take time to enjoy the journey. Allow yourself to be taken care of.

Kate types, "Holy shit, this is coming from your guides."

Mary responds with a crying emoji and then she sends back, "Gahhhhh. That is exactly what I needed to hear! I literally was thinking about water washing over my heart last night. And had this vision of an eagle lifting me up and into the dawn. "

"Are you freaking serious?!" Kate responds. Her heart is beating fast. The voice that came through was crystal clear. And writing the words felt like such a rush.

"I'm struggling with living with mom and dad, it's hard

to allow myself to be taken care of." Mary says.

The voice is back and words again flow out of Kate in a steady stream,

> The one who accepts help is the one who is able to give help in the future. By accepting help, you allow an exchange of energy to flow through your parents and to yourself. This help is what allows you to give back to the world tenfold in the future. You must learn this lesson of accepting grace so that you may be a beacon of grace for the future."

Mary sends another crying face emoji. "Gahhhhh… again, exactly what I needed to hear."

Kate leaned back in her chair with astonishment. She had never typed up anything like that before. What was once a whisper was now a choir of angels. And the eagle Mary had seen? Really, another eagle? This rush felt like Kate was in alignment with herself for the first time in a long time. What other kind of great wisdom could she access?

She closed her eyes and started a meditation where she only focused on her in and out breaths. As she drifted into the meditation, it was as though she lowered a mask and stood before a great veil. A veil that was the keeper of the physical world and a world of consciousness beyond any human comprehension. The veil was the keeper of the in-between. The place where all life intersects with Spirit. One need only become familiar with the veil to access it.

Kate didn't know it then, but one seemingly small exchange with her sister, was about to shift her entire perception of life. What she had thought was separate before and off limits to her, was actually not.

She pulled herself out of the meditation and texted Mary, "What in the actual F was that?" and a laughing emoji. "That was not from me. Things are literally coming through so clear for me right now."

Mary texted back, "Dude, how cool is this? You're totally connecting with my guides."

"I thought only you could do that," Kate sent back to Mary.

Mary texted, "Well, I journal with my guides and have random souls come to me all the time, but I don't come up with words like that for other people. Kate, I think you need to pay attention to what's happening here."

"Ummm, yeah, I would say so, LOL," Kate typed back.

Too excited to get back to work, Kate decided to go for a brief walk outside of her office.

Kate called back to Adler, "Hey, I'm going to take a quick walk, I'll be back."

Adler got up from her desk, "Ooh, can I join you?"

Before she meant to, Kate automatically responded, "Totally!" Kate was still buzzing with excitement.

Kate and Adler made their way outside towards the walking trail by their office. "Want to go this way, it's about 10 minutes around and then 10 minutes back to the office?" Kate said to Adler.

"Perfect" Adler said.

They started their walk along the trail and pulled their jackets up around themselves. It was cold.

"I'm so glad to have you working here this year. Since you started six months ago, things have been going so well,"Adler said to Kate.

"That means so much to me. Thank you for that." Kate said.

"I'm not ready for it to get this cold out," Adler zipped up her coat.

"Me neither."

They started walking along the trail and near a forest thicket, and Kate felt like she was buzzing from the inside out. Her mind could not stop thinking about the interaction between her and Mary. Had that really happened? She felt a pang of guilt go down to her ankles. She had been walking with Adler for five minutes before she even thought to ask her anything. Kate got along well with Adler and they liked to go running together after work some days.

Feeling like she hadn't been paying attention to Adler on the walk at all, she asked, "So what's going on with Jessie these days."

"Jessies's being Jessie. And I'm being me," Adler responded.

"Mm-hhmmm," Kate nodded, then asked, "How's that working out?"

"It's not" Adler laughed.

"Well, what's your plan?" Kate asked.

"Well he agreed we go to therapy together…"Adler started, but Kate didn't hear the rest of the sentence.

The voice she heard when she was texting her sister was back. And so was the vision of the hands.

"Thank you for taking care of me," Kate heard.

Kate focused in on the hands, they looked like Adler's holding someone else's hands.

Adler was still talking about her husband, Jessie, "I mean I guess it's worth a try, it didn't work last time though…"

Kate interrupted Adler, "I'm sorry. This is going to sound batshit crazy…"

Adler stopped walking and looked directly at Kate, "Huh?"

"Seriously, you can't judge me for this!" Kate paused for what seemed like the longest minute ever.

Adler broke the silence, staring intently at Kate, she could tell Kate was serious, and then she laughed, "Dude, what? Just spit it out."

"Did you used to hold your grandfather's hands?" Kate asked.

Adler was taken aback, "Uhmm?" was all she asked.

Kate swallowed. Just keep going she thought.

"Like before he died, did you used to go and sit with him and hold his hands?"

Adler's gaze pierced right into Kate's.

"When he got really sick, I'd go and sit with him and hold his hands at the nursing home."

"And they had age spots on them?" Kate interrupted.

Adler replied, "Uhmm, yeah, they were…"

"On the back of his hands, and he had a gold wedding ring?" Kate fired out.

"Yes." Adler looked intently at Kate with a shocked and puzzled look on her face.

"Okay, again, please don't judge me," Kate said.

"Dude!" Adler yelled back, laughing.

Kate went silent and fidgeted back and forth. Her heart swelled up into her throat as if it was on fire. Her hands were full of sweat.

Can I really say that I think I'm seeing her grandfather? Who am I to say something like this? She wondered.

The voice came back into her head and whispered, "Yes."

Before she could even think, the words slipped out of her mouth. "He's so thankful that you went to see him every day. And he's showing me how you would hold his hands."

"What do you mean he's showing you?" Adler asked, staring blankly at Kate.

"I can see his hands in my mind, I've been seeing them all morning," Kate nervously whispered back. "There are age spots on the back of them and he wears a simple gold wedding ring. The room is dimly lit, and he doesn't look like he has much time left. I keep hearing him say, 'Thank you, thank you.'"

Adler began to sob. "My papa passed away a year ago yesterday. The day before he passed, I sat with him and he would not stop saying thank you to me."

Kate's head and heart began to rush with excitement again. What was that? The trail they were walking on is about to hit the point where they reach the pine trees to turn back.

Adler's tears began to fade.

"You didn't know me last year when my papa was sick," Adler said.

"No, I didn't" Kate responded.

"Dude, you're a witch!" Adler laughed.

Kate laughed nervously, "I about threw up telling you that. I'm over here thinking I'm nuts."

"How did you know he had a gold wedding ring?" Adler asked.

"When I see the hands, he shows me the ring on them" Kate responded.

"Whoa." Adler says.

Kate gets another vision, this time of a pen with the Highland Nursing Home logo on it.

"Was he at Highland Nursing Home?" Kate asked.

"Yes." Said Adler, as her jaw dropped.

Kate's entire body softened into a peaceful trance as more visions, voices, and thoughts poured over her. It was as though she was being shown the entirety of Adler's relationship with her grandfather. The bond they shared. Kate's heart felt full of love and grief. It was as though she was in Adler's body, feeling what it must have been like to love her grandfather and lose him. The veil stood before Kate, completely open, like a mask that had been torn away. A knowing, technicolour feeling came into her heart.

"Thank you" Adler said as she gave Kate a hug. "Things have been so hard with Jessie lately, I am really struggling. And I miss my papa so much. He's been on my mind so heavy the last few days."

Adler and Kate reached the turnaround point on the trail.

"Let's head back to the office," Adler said.

"I'm in shock," Kate said.

"I am too!" Adler said. "I feel so grateful, holy cow, I really needed to hear all of that."

Kate answered, "I mean that was so crazy! I can't believe how clearly I saw all of that."

Adler was looking down at the trail. "You have a gift, dude!"

Adler noticed a piece of trash on the walking trail and bent to pick it up. She turned it over in her hand, "Hey, I thought this was trash, but this is kind of a neat sticker. Do you want it for your water bottle for running?" She turned to Kate, handing it to her.

On the sticker was an American flag with an eagle on it. Kate took the sticker and put it to her heart. The eagle had shown up again.

"Lyla, can you bring me your box of flies?" Kate yelled down to the waterfront.

Six-year-old Lyla was busy picking up stones and catching stoneflies and mayflies underneath the rocks at the banks of the river near the Jungle. The cool spring run-off of water into the Big Hole River was nearing its end, and the Jefferson River would soon drop in flow to provide ranchers with irrigation for the summer haying season. Fly fishing was in its prime, and Lyla was in her first season of fishing.

Kate knelt beside Lyla and helped her put her waders on, zipping them all the way up. "You ready to try your pole out today?" Kate asked.

"Yes, mommy!" Lyla excitedly said.

Kate had taken the day off from seeing clients for spiritual healing sessions to enjoy the summer solstice with a day of fishing at the Jungle. Her dad's footsteps came up behind her and he whispered, "Look over there."

Across the river high up in the cottonwood trees, a bald eagle had softly landed. The branch bent beneath his weight and swayed gently up and down.

"I haven't seen an eagle in ages!" Kate said excitedly.

Kate's eyes met with the eagle's and her heart leapt with excitement.

Are you ready? she heard in her head.

Always, Kate thought back.

Kate's eyes drifted to the crystal gurgling of the water. She could see mayflies darting side to side against the current. Her gaze fixated on the dance and the rhythm of the stream. She stepped out into the water with Lyla, and as the sound of their waders sloshed in the stream, Kate's mind flashed an image of her grandfather. She smiled gently. The water carried his spirit, as it had also carried her worries, all flowing in and out.

Kate looked over at Lyla and voiced an instruction. "You remember the flick movement to make?"

"Shhh, mommy, we're in the water!" Lyla whispered back to her mom.

Kate chuckled softly and listened closely to the rhythm of the stream. She could feel the veil, the in-between place, and she whispered back to her daughter, "Yes, yes, we are."

Kayla Lappin is a mom, wife, spiritual medium, spiritual coach, spiritual teacher, Reiki practitioner, yoga teacher, singer, writer, web-designer, environmental communicator, sister, daughter, and the list goes on. Labels aside, she is a Spiritual Medium who is passionate about helping people develop spiritual gifts to impact the world. Kayla lives in Butte, Montana.

SIX

WHENEVER I CLOSE MY EYES

Jerry Kustich

A T MY AGE I no longer chase dreams, but feel fortunate that at one time, I did. Growing up in the fifties on an island in the Niagara River, I remember those years with great fondness. "The River," as we called it, flowed from Lake Erie, over Niagara Falls, and into Lake Ontario. It was a critical influence during the formative years of my youth.

Although the Niagara was a polluted mess at the time, I roamed the shoreline and caught some fish while wading through the green fetid slime that piled upon its bank. Realizing that something was not right, childhood dreams of pristine rivers with big fish were piqued by stories in *Outdoor Life* and various other sporting magazines. However, those remote destinations seemed otherworldly and out of reach for a young kid. And though I left "The River" behind at eighteen to pursue adulthood, its impact lingered as life continued to unfold.

After several years of twists, turns and misdirections, it took the turmoils of the late sixties and early seventies for me to understand the importance of living near a river once again. Striving for new goals that were not earth-shattering in a society defined by financial success, like a modern-day Siddhartha, I set out to find a liquid dream of peace, contentment, and meaning that would not only flow through my soul, but also renew my spirit while inspiring a life of simplicity.

There are those who say our lives are a sum total of one's choices, but I say sometimes dumb luck, fate, or even a guiding force plays a part as well. Whatever the reason, one must be prepared to follow a path that makes sense when the opportunity arises. I consider myself blessed to have found what I was looking for along the way. Most significantly, I can revisit that special past whenever I close my eyes.

The decision to move to southwestern Montana to be near the Big Hole River was made somewhere in Nebraska on I-80. My wife Debra and I were returning from a visit with family and doing some fishing in Western New York in mid-October 1983, when spontaneous concocted a plan. The plan was inspired by several camping trips we had taken to Montana since our marriage in 1980. For me, it was all about the fishing. For Debra, however, it was the connection of the region to the Lewis and Clark Expedition that excited her.

I met Debra during a weekend Forest Service picnic at Powell Ranger Station on the Idaho side of Lolo Pass during the summer of 1979. In the shadow of the Selway-Bitterroot Wilderness area, we both worked there as seasonal employees. Normally, I didn't participate in such gatherings but fate had a different plan for me that day. Unfortunately, the day before the picnic, I had rolled and totaled my personal pick-up truck while en route to Montana for a weekend of fishing. Consequently, I had no choice but to hang around. I felt lucky to still be alive.

Debra took the opportunity to introduce herself and offer sympathy for my unfortunate mishap that had to do with of having too little sleep the night before the accident and being overly enthusiastic about casting my fly that evening in Rock Creek, east of Missoula, instead of taking a nap. During our conversation I learned that Debra was a full-time teacher in the Bay Area working at a prominent school for dyslexics. Additionally, during her summer breaks for the past two years, she had been working on a special project to reestablish the Lewis and Clark trail throughout the entire Powell Ranger District.

Using historic maps, notes, and landmarks, Debra was visibly thrilled talking about wandering the ridge tops alone and retracing the steps of the Expedition. She was documenting the updated version of the explorers' journey. For her efforts, she not only got paid, but the project was to be her Master's thesis from the University of Montana. And though we seemed to connect on various levels, it would be two weeks before we randomly bumped into each other again.

While waiting for my insurance claim to be settled, I borrowed my boss's old pickup and camper for yet another attempt at a weekend getaway to Montana. Turning onto Highway 12 from the Forest Service compound driveway with the enthusiastic anticipation that trout fishing generates, I was taken by surprise to see Debra on the side of the road, hitchhiking. With no hesitation, of course, I pulled over and offered her a ride. She happily accepted, so together we chugged off to Missoula. After another engaging conversation, Debra volunteered to buy a sleeping bag in town so that she could spend the entire weekend with me camping at Rock Creek. Some things in life are simply meant to be.

During my time working seven-month seasons at Powell in central Idaho I would spend winters living off-grid in the remote woods of northern Idaho. After reading *Trout Fishing* by Joe Brooks, the editor of *Outdoor Life,* in the early seventies, I was inspired to follow my fishing dreams. Joe was a fly-fishing pioneer who wrote about destinations like Alaska, Canada, Europe, Argentina, and even Montana in an era when world fishing travel was uncommon.

Upon reading the section in his book about a trout oddly named the Dolly Varden, I became intrigued. As I continued my ongoing effort to reset my life in the mid seventies, finding a Dolly Varden became my mantra, and I left my current residence in Salt Lake City to embark on the search. Living in my truck camper for a few weeks I searched Montana and Idaho until I met someone who knew someone who guided me to a stream where I caught a Dolly, near the town of Priest River, Idaho.

Coincidentally, I also discovered that my uncle from Buffalo, New York, had tragically died in a Civilian Conservation Corps accident near Priest River in the 1930s. It felt as if destiny had guided me to buy a few acres of land and construct a rustic cabin on a small brook trout creek north of town.

Working at Powell Ranger Station for four years in the late seventies allowed further exploration of places detailed in *Trout Fishing*. Joe wrote about cutthroat trout, which I regularly caught in the beautiful Lochsa River that flowed through the ranger district. However, it was the section in the book on page 46, discussing the Montana grayling, that ignited a new desire within me. As it happened, Joe loved the Big Hole River and spent much time there. He noted that one could find this unique species in the upper reaches of the Big Hole near the town of Wisdom. So that's where I headed one weekend in 1977.

Before going, I conducted research on grayling and discovered that they were introduced into several rivers in Montana and Michigan after the glaciers receded thousands of years ago. But now, the only viable natural population of grayling in the lower forty-eight states exists in the Big Hole. Officially considered a threatened species, fishery managers have been working creatively to keep them off the endangered list, considering the potential negative consequences it could have on local communities. To this day the population hangs on due to the singular features of the Upper Big Hole that resemble the low-gradient cold rivers of the Arctic. These very traits have also facilitated the survival of the introduced eastern brook trout. Despite the coexistence of both species, the brook trout is still regarded as an ongoing threat to the well-being of the native grayling.

After landing my first grayling on July 2, 1977, the upper Big Hole Valley hooked me. It was enchanting in many ways. Like stepping back in time, remnants of the Wild West seemed to live on within its mystical aura of vastness. Cowboys, cattle, picturesque hayfields and even an expanse of open land accented by the meandering river held a mesmerizing power over my wandering soul. As an undefinable spirit rose up to touch me, I immediately realized that I had found the special river I had been seeking. In the years that followed, embarking on camping trips to discover the wonders of the Big Hole River became a routine mission.

After our spontaneous camping trip in the summer

of 1979, Debra and I fell in love. Following that, I spent the following winter with her in the Bay Area south of San Francisco, and even taught math part-time at her school. As part of my unique contract, I was granted time to indulge in ocean fishing off the jetty in Half Moon Bay every Wednesday, and I never missed a day. Debra was the ultimate tree-hugger, so we spent much of our free time exploring the outdoors and watching birds up and down the coast. However, when the time arrived to renew her contract for the following year, she ultimately chose to forego her California lifestyle and join me in my humble cabin in Idaho. Following my retirement from the Forest Service, I dedicated numerous hours to teaching and tutoring throughout the summer at her school. Finally, at the end of August 1980, we tied the knot and relocated up north. As September drew to a close, we took our honeymoon, spending it camping first at Rock Creek and then at the Upper Big Hole.

Since we didn't have any children, our unconventional lifestyle living off-grid with virtually no expenses allowed us to travel around the continent frequently camp in Montana. Debra taught dyslexia workshops and we both tutored a month or two during the summers in California for a few years to support our modest lifestyle in Idaho.

So when we decided to move near the Big Hole while driving through Nebraska that October, we had stashed more than enough money for a down payment. At first Sheridan near the Ruby River was on our radar, but then the real estate agent showed us a quaint, affordable house in Twin Bridges with a greenhouse attached that seemed perfect, so we bought it. The whole deal took about an hour. And since one of the twin bridges spanned the Big Hole less than two miles away, we couldn't have been happier.

The plan was to move into our house the following spring after spending winter in our wonderful north woods cabin, But to our dismay, upon our return to Idaho in early November, we found that our homey abode had been completely ransacked and robbed. Clothes, utensils, furniture, boat, guitar—all were gone. Despite our shock and anger, we were thankful that we had just bought a house in Montana. It took a few weeks to scavenge the few items left behind along with saying our fond goodbyes to a sentimental past before heading back to where our new home awaited in Twin Bridges. We never looked back.

On their search for water passage to the Pacific, the Lewis and Clark Expedition took the river flowing from the west where three major river forks came together to form the Missouri River. They named that river Jefferson. Included in their crew of about forty members was the Lemhi Shoshone woman Sacagawea who had been kidnapped by a warring native tribe when she was twelve. Sold to the French-Canadian explorer Toussaint Charbonneau to become his wife, they both joined the Expedition in Fort Mandan. Charbonneau would be the interpreter for the party and pregnant Sacagawea would be a guide to her homeland where they all potentially needed to go.

In early August, 1805, Lewis led a small scouting party up the Jefferson River until they came upon three additional major tributaries. Meanwhile, Clark and the rest of the crew were days behind negotiating the canoes upstream. While Lewis camped on the middle fork, Clark took the west fork instead. Because that fork was too difficult to navigate, Clark decided to retreat and fortunately met up with Lewis and his small crew on the middle fork. The east fork, which is now the Ruby River, they named Philanthropy. The west fork, which is now the Big Hole, they named Wisdom. They decided to continue up the middle fork after Sacagawea recognized a landmark of outcropping rocks resembling a beaver's head. Although the party continued to call the middle fork Jefferson, it was eventually renamed Beaverhead River after its prominent landmark.

Presently, it is believed that the approximate location of Lewis and Clark's campsite is situated near the Madison County fairgrounds on the outskirts of Twin Bridges. In commemoration, a life-size bronze statue of Sacagawea carrying her baby, created by friend and artist Dick Crane, now stands in a place of honor on the fairgrounds.

As the expedition moved further upstream Sacagawea was able to guide the party to her Lemhi Shoshone people. With winter nearing, and snow in the mountains, finding a safe way westward then became a critical concern. Upon crossing the Continental Divide through Lemhi Pass, the Expedition relied on Shoshone guidance. When it was determined that taking the Salmon River flowing westward would be too treacherous, they embarked on a rugged overland trail. Over the Sula mountains and down the Bitterroot River Valley, a Shoshone guide led the crew to Lolo Creek where they began the challenging upward trek over Lolo Pass. Once on the other side of the pass, dropping down to navigate what is now known as the Lochsa River was deemed to be a mistake.

With snow getting deeper, food in short supply, the waters of the Lochsa too rough, and the valley too tight to follow on foot, the expedition was dangerously bogged down near where the Powell Ranger Station now stands. They famously resorted to killing a colt for sustenance before finding an escape route from the deep valley and making their way up to Wendover Ridge, where they continued their westward journey. This is the trail that Debra retraced and documented for historical accuracy, and it is near Colt Killed Creek where we had met that weekend in 1979.

It was early December when we arrived at the house awaiting us in Twin Bridges. Both Debra and I felt immediately connected to the town, but for different reasons. Although our first two weeks were spent in record-cold temperatures, local neighbors helped us gather enough firewood to survive the frigid temperatures. When the weather finally broke in late December, I was even able to fish the icy edge of the lower Big Hole near town for the first time. This would be the beginning of countless outings exploring the entire river from my home over the next three decades.

Flowing 150 miles east, then south, then east and then west in a gigantic S-shape from its headwaters above Wisdom, the river changes directions as well as character several times until its confluence with the Beaverhead to form the Jefferson River one mile north of Twin Bridges. To me the Big Hole represents the quintessential free-flowing wild trout river like I had read about when I was a kid, and I intended to fish as much of it as possible.

Eventually Debra set up a well-respected tutoring business for learning disabled students throughout southwestern Montana, while becoming heavily involved with both the local library and the regional Audubon chapter. In the spring of 1984 I met the owners of Winston Rod, Glenn Brackett and Tom Morgan, and since they were expanding business and hiring at the time, I was at the right place at the right time to get the job. And though it was only part-time to begin with, they expected me to use the flexibility of the position to fish as much as possible while getting acquainted with the local waters. The opportunity led to four decades of rod building and lifetime of fishing.

Remembrances connected to fishing the Big Hole are too numerous to recount. From top to bottom, I explored most of it, and though I rarely fished the river from a boat, I learned all the walk-in spots in any direction from the town of Twin Bridges. There was easy-to-get-to water up the Burma Road over Pennington Bridge to Glen, which I often visited.

I would also take the twenty-mile bench road to Melrose giving access to Maiden Rock Canyon and all of the upper sections of the river as well. Over time, fishing the canyon well into dark became a passion, especially after I caught my personal-best river brown trout in the late eighties with my brother, who was visiting at the time. That gravel track induced many flat tires over the years and I resorted to carrying two spares: just in case. The regular trek was always worth the effort despite having to change a tire now and then on a dusty remote backroad in the dark void of midnight.

For me, the Big Hole was always unpredictable and moody, but then that challenge added to its mysterious charm. Being a free-flowing river, water levels and temperatures always varied, but eventually I learned where to be for midges in March, Skwallas and baetis in April, Mother's Day caddis in May, salmonflies in June, PMDs and yellow sallies in July, tricos and hoppers in August, and red quills in September. And when all else failed, swinging soft hackles at dusk often enticed a few nice fish. As time passed I found some consistent "secret" spots that included a couple of very productive side channels.

On those days when I only had an hour or two to fish, the water just outside of town offered intriguing possibilities. Though fish populations had been scant there for a couple of decades due to low water caused by draw down for irrigation, the fishing pressure was low as well. And despite it all, there were always a few fish to be found—especially in the spring and fall.

Perhaps the most attractive allure of the Big Hole was the primal spirit that emanates from just being in its presence, and fly fishing was the pathway to get there. Like the heartbeat of the universe, the pulsing rhythm of a river can balance mind, heart, body and soul as it holistically heals a broken spirit. I found this to be especially true with the Big Hole. When my friend Norm visited from Florida one April in the early 2000s, we walked up the lower river and shared a mystical day of fishing. Recovering from a serious medical procedure at the time, he still remembers that experience as a turning point in his total healing process. Little did I realize then how much I would need that same blessing again a few years later.

For local communities, the intrinsic value and special nature of the Big Hole as a unifying force has never been taken for granted. The people of Anaconda and Butte have long had a standing love affair with the river, thanks in part to pioneer environmentalist and Butte native George Grant. As a visionary, George Grant preached river conservation way back in the 1930s, but his near-single-handed effort to stop the construction of the Reichle Dam in 1975 was his crowning achievement. Preaching the merit of a free flowing trout river at a time when such a concept was considered un-American, he prevented a ten-mile stretch of the Big Hole from becoming a reservoir. Subsequently, he also later fought for stream access, stream bed protection, and a ten mile slot limit regulation through Maiden Rock Canyon. To commemorate his lifelong commitment to the river, Butte's Trout Unlimited Chapter was renamed for George Grant in the early eighties.

When a long section of the Jefferson River dried up in 1988 during an extended three year drought as the lower Big Hole River upstream was nearly sucked dry as well by desperate irrigators, it was the George Grant TU Chapter that led the way negotiating with conservation-minded ranchers up and down the river. Eventually agreements were made that led to widespread in-stream flow legislation meant to prevent catastrophic events like this from ever recurring in the future.

Thanks to the concerned citizens of Butte, the Big Hole was again saved. In the early nineties, concerned sport folks throughout the Ruby Valley, including Twin Bridges, were inspired to set up a Trout Unlimited chapter, named after Lewis and Clark. This chapter aimed to closely monitor the condition of our local water bodies, from the Ruby River to the lower Big Hole, lower Beaverhead, and upper Jefferson Rivers. Getting intensely involved with Trout Unlimited was the least I could do for the rivers I loved. Despite feeling somewhat like an outsider when I adopted the Big Hole River as my home river, I hoped to repay it in my own small way for everything it had meant to me.

Over the decades my job-related fishing travels expanded to various locations across the continent, including regular visits to the reclaimed Niagara River of my youth. However, the Big Hole always stayed close to my heart. In April, 2006, it was an honor to start up Sweetgrass Rods with legendary bamboo rod maker Glenn Brackett. Realizing travel time would be limited until the company got up and running, fishing local water became more important than ever. And because of Trout Unlimited's effort to provide consistent in-stream flow for the lower Big Hole, the fish population had increased significantly the previous decade, making fishing the local section even more enticing.

When Debra was diagnosed with ALS in August, 2006, we were devastated. With no good prognosis the inevitable was just a matter of a couple years. For me, hiking up the Big Hole with the few fragments of time I then had available was not only comforting, but I also gained an inner strength that I was able to share with Debra throughout our ordeal. Reaffirming that the most important aspect of any river is not just the opportunity to catch a fish, but the spiritual energy that flows from just being there, I relied on that more than ever after Debra died on March 17, 2009.

Since Debra requested that her ashes be released into the Lochsa River, the following summer I took our last drive together over Lewis and Clark's historic Lolo Pass and down past where I first picked her up hitchhiking to Missoula in 1979. Finding the perfect place on the Lochsa very near where we had met, I released her remains into its riffles as I watched them solemnly flow toward eternity.

In tearful solitude, I stood. Always living with the belief that some things are meant to be, this was a time I wished they were not.

In 2013 it was time to move on, start another chapter far from Montana, and explore new water. Greek philosopher Heraclitus once stated that "No man ever steps into the same river twice," but I contend that we can remember a river–the same–forever. And though I no longer live near the Big Hole, it will continue to flow through my dreams whenever I close my eyes.

Jerry Kustich is a former owner of Sweetgrass Rods. He also authored At the River's Edge: Lessons Learned in a Life of Fly Fishing, A Wisp in the Wind: In Search of Bull Trout, Bamboo, and Beyond, *and* Fly Fishing for Great Lakes Steelhead. *His latest book is* Around the Next Bend: A Fly Angler's Journey. *His articles and essays have appeared in* Fly Fisherman, Big Sky Journal, Fly Rod & Reel, *and many other publications.*

SEVEN

PARDNERS AND DOGS

Paul Vang

IN THE MOVIE VERSION of the Broadway musical comedy, *Paint Your Wagon*, a young Clint Eastwood plays the role of Pardner, the young man that Lee Marvin's character, Ben Rumson, takes under his wing to teach him the ins and outs of the California Gold Rush. Only at the end of the show do we learn Pardner's actual name, Sylvester Newel, which Rumson scorns as a farmer's name, though he concedes that Pardner was the best pardner he ever had. Like Ben Rumson, pardners have been a big part of my life too.

I grew up on a farm in southern Minnesota, and we had good neighbors. Hank was a neighboring farmer and both he and my dad liked to go fishing. It got confusing at times. Both neighbor Hank and my dad were named Henry, and both Henrys got called Hank. Hank had three sons and a daughter, Beverly (I would cheerfully admit to being smitten with Bev from an early age. She was even born on Valentine's Day). I don't recall Bev coming along on fishing outings, but Hank and one or two of his sons joined us on many fishing trips on those occasional days when rain interfered with farm work. If Hank didn't come fishing, we still had three, Dad, my brother Carl, and me, as a fishing group.

Years later, after finishing college and beginning a career with the Social Security Administration, I had a good thing going at work. Among the twenty or so people who worked at the office, we had a core group of guys, mostly at the beginning of our marriages and careers. We had common interests, with pheasant hunting being near the top of the list. When opening weekend came, pheasants were the center of conversation at lunch and coffee breaks. By the end of the workweek, we'd generally have a carload of four or five lined up for that opening day hunt. One year, on Friday, the day before the season opened, Bill called in sick. We had an emergency planning meeting. George, ever the pessimist, groaned, "Oh, he won't be able to hunt tomorrow."

Still, at 6 a.m., the next morning, when the carpool pulled up at Bill's house, Bill came out the door with his gear, threw it in the trunk, and climbed in. When asked about his health, Bill was matter of fact, "I wasn't that damned sick."

George, incidentally, while the eternal pessimist, turned out to be a big winner. The Heinz company had a sweepstakes one year. To enter, all you had to do was put your name and address on the back of a Heinz soup can label and mail it in. For something like four months or so, George faithfully had the contents from a can of a Heinz soup in his thermos every day for lunch and sent in the label. At the end of the year, darned if George wasn't one of the winners, and his prize was a brand-new Ford Falcon convertible, the color of a Heinz soup label. We immediately proclaimed George's new car the perfect car for road-hunting for pheasants.

In fact, that following October, the gang piled into

George's spiffy Heinz-red Falcon for the pheasant opener. In the afternoon it was warm enough to put the top down and dang! One of the guys actually shot a rooster pheasant sitting on top of a fencepost from the back seat of the convertible. I think it was even legal under 1960's North Dakota regulations.

Fishing was more of a family thing. My wife, Kay, enjoyed fishing from a boat, and it was easy to go to one of many lakes in the area and rent a boat for the day. I was able to buy a used Johnson 5 ½ horse outboard motor, too. Then babies came along, and for a few years, Kay was tied down, so I'd often get up before dawn on Saturday mornings to go fishing and would usually be home by noon, or so, with several fish that I'd converted to fillets.

Good things never last. As promotion opportunities came up, one by one, the office group became individuals going in different directions. While more job transfers got in the way of developing hunting or fishing partners, I did something better: I raised my own partner. Our son, Kevin, was about five years old when he started tagging along on those Iowa pheasant hunts.

Eventually, job transfers brought us to Montana, and a longtime interest in fly fishing found its way to the top. The Big Hole River was just half an hour from our back door, not to mention the many other streams, small and large along the Continental Divide. I stopped in at the local fly-shop and got acquainted with the owner and some of the store regulars. We moved in the dead of winter, so fishing wasn't too important to start with, but by March we had a nice weekend and I drove out in search of fishing water on the Ruby River. Amazingly, at the first place I stopped, the landowner graciously gave me permission to fish. Fishing was slow, though I remember catching a whitefish, sluggish in the ice-cold winter water. I looked around, marveling at the snow-capped mountains peaks and had to pinch myself. I'm fishing in Montana, I thought. I'm not even on vacation; I live here.

In those first few years, I got into a kaffeeklatsch at a restaurant near my office, so I got to be friends with a group of guys who were Butte natives. John Banovich shared my interests in hunting and fishing. Almost exactly ten years older than me, he had recently retired and his sons had moved away. There were local grandsons, though they were tied up in athletics and didn't have much time for outings with their grandfather.

We'd go on an occasional day of fishing or hunting, and we clicked. John had connections going back for decades, and he introduced me to rancher friends on whose properties he'd hunted and fished for years. Suddenly, I had access to private land, though I never went to those properties unless we were going together. One of the basic rules of hunting and fishing with another person is to respect that person's access to private property and not abuse the privilege.

John had a wealth of knowledge about local hunting and fishing. While he'd had a long career with a utility company, he occasionally moonlighted as a fishing guide for Fran Johnson, himself a legendary character, who was a guide for many years and then opened a sporting goods store. John had fished just about everywhere, and hunted for deer, elk, moose, and waterfowl in our corner of Montana.

After a few more years, I reached age 55, and by that time had over 30 years of employment in the federal government, so I was able to retire. John approved of that idea, suggesting that, "Now that you're through f---ing around at the Social Security Office, maybe we can get in some hunting and fishing."

And we did, indeed, pick up the pace of trips together. A highlight of those trips was conversations on the way to and from our destinations. He was full of stories about long-ago hunts, about characters he'd known, and if talk got boring, he might burst into a song from an opera.

With John as my mentor, I got my first couple elk while he got his last couple elk. I got several white-tailed deer, thanks to John's landowner contacts. I especially got a kick out of John when the real work began after that deer or elk was down. I'd get down on my knees and ready to open that carcass when John would growl, "Ah, get out of the way, you're just going to f--- it up." He would take over the field dressing process and, give him credit, he'd do a beautiful job of it. I thought I knew how to field dress a deer, but I learned a lot from watching him.

Times change. After about seven or eight years of regular outings, John's health declined and I'm sorry to say, our partnership kind of faded away. There was never a cross word or break in our friendship, but I was back to square one as far as any kind of partnership was concerned.

Besides human pardners, there have been other constant companions through the years: our dogs. In 1970, Sam, a black Labrador retriever puppy, became part of our family. Sam (for Samantha) was a great "starter" dog. She was easy to train, and was a soft-mouthed, reliable retriever for ducks, pheasants, and grouse. On our annual summer vacations, she loved to keep me company while I fished the streams.

Sam lived a long life, going on one last grouse hunt on Columbus Day of 1984. By then, she was kind of just going through the motions of hunting, mostly content to tag along with me. However, I do remember she picked up the scent of a bird and flushed it. She died in her sleep just a few days later.

Our next Lab was Alix, a chocolate Labrador retriever. She was just a pup when she had her first exposure to fly fishing on our annual summer vacation in the mountains. It was our first morning in camp and I got up early to do a little fishing while my wife slept in.

I'd built a new flyrod over the previous winter, using a then-new variation on fiberglass flyrods, graphite. It was a 9-foot 5-weight rod, a replacement for my first flyrod, one I'd built from a Herter's rod kit, which had fatally splintered in the previous season. I was putting the two sections together, under Alix's supervision. The tip end of the rod passed near her snout, and she reached out and bit off the first few inches. I don't remember if I had any nasty words for her or not. I trimmed off the rod at the first guide and went fishing. It fished just fine, though after we got home, I ordered a new tip section and rebuilt it that winter.

Alix had a nose for deer, going back to when she was a pup demonstrating a keen nose for finding and eating deer droppings. When we hunted pheasants in a river bottom, she also had a knack for sniffing out big whitetail bucks. When she'd get bored watching me fly fishing, she'd often disappear off into the riparian trees and brush. She'd come when called, but the next day I'd often find some deer hooves she'd regurgitated. Yes, she had a nose for deer.

John Banovich thought the world of Alix, especially after seeing her retrieving some ducks that had fallen in thick cover at the edge of a warm-water creek.

John and I were together hunting grouse in early September of 1997, when Alix collapsed, gasping for air. After several minutes she got her wind back, but on this warm, early fall day, we decided she'd better not do any more work that day.

As weather cooled, she had some good hunts, but her stamina continued to decline.

On the way home from the opening weekend of pheasant season we stopped at the home of a Lab breeder we had contacted after seeing a newspaper want ad. During the drive, my wife and I discussed names for this black puppy curled up on my lap while she drove. I suggested we name her Candy because she was so sweet.

Candy had to grow up quickly as Alix's health declined. By Thanksgiving weekend, we reached the point where Alix had to stay home while Candy took over the bird dog chores. We said goodbye to Alix that winter.

The problem with dogs as hunting and fishing partners is that, sooner or later, we have to say goodbye to them. After Candy, we had another black Lab named Flicka, and now we have Kiri, our fifth Labrador retriever. Kiri is now seven years old, and I occasionally speculate whether she'll be our last dog. For that matter, I sometimes speculate which of us will have to say goodbye, this time.

All these Labs had their own individual personalities and quirks, but they all shared a deep happiness to be with their people and an eagerness to accompany us on outings, whether it was a walk around the block, a day along a river, or searching for grouse in the aspens or pheasants on the prairies.

Not everybody agrees with having a dog as a fishing partner. I recall a mini tempest in the now defunct Fly

Rod & Reel magazine, which ran an ad showing a Lab with an angler. I don't recall what the ad was selling, but some readers sent letters to the editor complaining about anglers bringing their dogs along on outings, claiming it ruined the day for other people. They have a point, but it seems to me that the only outings my dogs have ever ruined have been mine, rarely anyone else's.

Flicka was a handful as a pup, and after our first fishing outings together, I began to question whether I'd ever catch another fish, as every time I'd cast my fly, she'd run out to retrieve it. That retrieving instinct is why we have Labs, but it can be trying at times. Candy, for her part, loved sticks. When I was in the river fishing, I could depend on Candy coming to me with a stick that she wanted me to throw. I'd try to ignore her, but eventually I'd give up and throw it for her, and that meant it would come back for me to throw again. And again. And again.

Kiri's special power is finding sandals or boot soles along the edge of the rivers I'm fishing. I never realized how many people evidently finish outings with one bare foot, or with a boot that lost a sole (not to be confused with its soul). When Kiri does find one of these treasures, she likes to show it to me as her trophy as well as telling me that this sandal or boot sole is also a good retrieving toy.

Another of her superpowers is perching herself on a big rock in a river. I don't know how many photos I now have on the theme of "Dog on a Rock," but it's a lot and the collection keeps growing.

In short, having my dog along as my fishing partner is a never-ending source of smiles and laughs, the stuff of happy memories. Of course, having a dog along on spring and summer angling outings means that in autumn, when we turn our attention to the aspen thickets and prairies in search of grouse and pheasants, my canine partner is ready to go. I don't pretend to be a great dog trainer, but whatever shortcomings my dogs have had over the years, it has never been a lack of interest in going out on yet another outing.

But I'm content. I truly enjoy a day of fly fishing on my favorite river or chasing pheasants across the prairie with nobody to talk to except Kiri. We don't have to check each other's calendars, or worry about whose turn it is to drive, or how to split gas costs on a longer trip. She always likes my choice of sandwiches and never groans when I tell a dumb joke.

I still miss John, my old hunting and fishing friend and pardner. He was unique and I'll never have another partner like him. I'm already about ten years older than he was when he mostly gave up hunting and fishing. For that matter, I'm the last survivor of that old kaffeeklatsch of guys where I met John.

I'm not oblivious to the inescapable fact that one of these days my fly fishing and hunting days will come to an end. When that day arrives, I envision it ending with an old man and his old dog emerging from the dusk after sunset, with a fly rod or shotgun in hand and a happy smile.

In addition to weekly newspaper columns, Paul Vang has been published in many magazines, including Montana Outdoors, North Dakota Outdoors, Kiwanis, Wheelin' Sportsmen, Blue Ridge, *and* Distinctly Montana. *He has won awards from the Outdoor Writers Association of America and Montana Newspaper Association. Paul and his wife, Kay, and black Lab, Kiri, live in Butte, Montana.*

EIGHT

∽

GALLERY OF PHOTOGRAPHY

Photos by Tim Foster

*Alex Kielburger and Jon Foster
of Wild Valley Supply Co.
enjoying a warm autumn day
out on the river and SUP fly fishing in
Annapolis Valley, Nova Scotia.*

∽

*Wisdom River cover image is also
by Tim Foster.*

Tim Foster

Tim Foster

NINE

HOW YOU FELLAS MAKING OUT?

Greg Allard

It's Rich; he's calling me to confirm the details of tomorrow's trip. "The guy's name is Dave. Pick him up at the Alma at nine."

"Okay, sounds good," I reply.

"And bring all the gear. He didn't bring his rod or anything," Rich adds.

"You know that's a late start. We're going to miss the early morning Stonefly fishing. We should be on the water by six a.m," I say.

"Yeah, I know, but he's flying in late, and that's when he'll be ready to go."

I sigh in frustration and say, "Yeah, okay, whatever."

Rich is my guiding partner. He's a retired Air Force jet mechanic who spent twenty-five years keeping Canada's fleet of F-18s combat-ready and a couple of years flying around with the Canadian Forces Snowbirds, the 431 Flying Demonstration Squadron. Rich is a no nonsense, "get er' done" kind of guy, with a big heart and a great sense of humor. Most of his season is spent guiding fly-in clients for an all-inclusive week of fly fishing. They spend four days drifting on the Bow River and a couple of days fishing the Mountain streams for cutthroat trout. I take care of the rest of the clients: the single-day float trips, walk-and-wade outings, and evening dry fly hunts.

The Alma is a contemporary, Euro-styled hotel located on the University of Calgary campus. Some of the visiting professors, lecturer's and researchers are offered a recreational day, compliments of the University. They can choose a sightseeing bus tour to Banff, birdwatching in Fish Creek Provincial Park, concerts, or a guided fly-fishing walk-and-wade outing on the lower Bow River. That's where I come in.

Rich prefers clients who are hardcore fly fishers looking to land a trophy trout of a lifetime, and he will work his butt off for a week straight to make it happen. He usually succeeds in that regard. The "brainiacs," as he might refer to them, well, he would rather that I deal with them, or anyone from the liberal arts crowd for that matter.

We finish our brief chat and hang up. I check the weather forecast for tomorrow. Sunny, high of 28 C (82 F), Wind SW 40 km/hr. gusting to 60 km/hr. (25 to 40 mph), late in the morning. *Good grief*, I think. *It's going to be a tough day on the water. I hope the client can cast well.*

It's 8:45 a.m. when I roll up to the lobby doors. Dave is already waiting. I get out of my car to greet and welcome him to Calgary. "It looks like it's going to be a great day," I lie. He seems nice, in his early seventies, relaxed and easy-going. "UCLA," he tells me on the drive to the river. Dave is a neurosurgeon and researcher who grew up fishing the streams of the Sans Gabriel Mountains of California. He loves fishing dry flies but hates fishing nymphs and bobbers. With six decades of fly fishing experience, he's caught plenty of trout and doesn't care much about numbers anymore. It's mid-July and the Calgary Stampede is bringing in 100,000 tourists a day, so the river will be busy.

I need to find a spot away from the walk-and-wade traffic in the city and the sometimes-endless stream of drift boats. I drive south to the edge of the city limits. Most of the boats that launched early at Fish Creek will have passed by hours ago, so we should have some peace and quiet. Hopefully, the wind stays reasonable for the rest of the morning. Fingers crossed. Dave and I talk about fly fishing on the drive to the river. He mentions having some mobility issues, so he can't walk too far. I explain that the Bow River can be a difficult river to fish at times, and changing conditions can quickly put the fish down.

I pull over next to the "No Parking" sign at the bridge on Highway 2, which puts us as close to the water as I can get. After a short walk, we reach the first pool, and apart from the faint background rumble of highway traffic, we are out of the urban jungle and have the bank to ourselves. I quickly rig up a fly and hand the rod to Dave.

"We're going to try fishing with a large foam Stonefly pattern," I explain. "The female golden stoneflies are egg laying through the night and early morning at this time of the season and maybe we can still find some trout to come up for the large dry fly," I lie, again. I know that we are probably too late for the Stonefly action and it's just too bright and sunny for the trout to commit to an eat on the surface this late in the morning without a major hatch to entice them. But, maybe we'll get lucky, and there's still plenty of day left to be optimistic. So here we are, fishing on a sunny, warm July morning on the Bow River. So far so good.

Now, to be a great walk-and-wade fishing guide, it's important to remember to keep your mouth shut, especially when the client first starts fishing. They have come from afar to fish the blue-ribbon Bow and the last thing they want to hear is some guide criticizing their every cast. I simply let them get into the Zen of the moment, to enjoy the smell of summer on the fresh morning breeze, to listen to the sound of the river, the birds singing, time to let the mind wander, for the river to cast its spell and the magic to happen. Be quiet!

I take a minute to assess the conditions around me. There aren't many insects floating in the drift yet, and no golden stones to be seen. A small flock of gulls are sitting on a gravel bar, many pruning themselves and one appears to be sleeping. I spot a pair of Mallard hens with a large brood of ducklings huddled in a slack-water pool along the shoreline. The younger, first-year hens often share motherhood with an older hen and combine their broods. However, sometimes, the young hen will abandon the family, leaving the older hen to raise all the ducklings on her own. The drakes usually gather and stay away from the hens once the hens start incubating their eggs, and play no role in rearing. Some people are a lot like Mallards.

The wind is moderate, from the southeast, blowing upstream and slightly off our bank. I expect it to turn to the southwest when it picks up, as the forecast said it would, and soon. I'm worried that it will be a tough day for dry fly fishing.

Dave strips line off the reel and starts to present his fly along the edges of the current seam and works slowly and methodically upriver, through the long pool. His casting is decent, and he's focused, but not rushed. The first hour sneaks by uneventfully. I suggest a fly change to Dave, something with a little extra flash on it to get the fish's attention through the broken water of the riffles. He likes the concept, and I remind him to stay hydrated as it is getting very warm, and the sun's glare off the water is intense. He is in good spirits and seems to be enjoying his adventure.

Dave turns back to the water with the new fly and renewed hope. "What are those? Pelicans?" Dave asks in amazement. Two adult American White Pelicans come drifting down the river. "Yes indeed," I reply. "They come for the summer to breed and rear their young. In September, they will fly back to the Gulf of Mexico in Texas to spend the winter," I explain. "I didn't know that they came this far north, all the way up to Canada," Dave says. "Well, the pelicans only showed up in Alberta and on the Bow River in 1974, a year after Calgary's Sam Livingston Fish Hatchery started a lake-stocking program," I explain. "With stocked fingerling trout in almost every pothole lake in southern Alberta, word traveled quickly through the migratory bird kingdom and now, thirty-five years later, here they are. Every single one of those large adult pelicans eats four pounds of my Bow River fish, every day. That's about five hundred pounds total, each season," I protest.

I always try to point out the local wildlife that we may encounter to my guests. What might seem like a normal, common wildlife sighting to me may be a once-in-a-lifetime moment for a visiting angler from another country or continent. Southern Alberta is a land of wild, natural abundance. The Bow River is home to bald eagles, ospreys, peregrine falcons, red-tailed hawks, ducks, pheasants, Canada geese, great horned owls, great gray owls, mink, beavers, kingfishers, black bears, bobcats, coyotes, and occasionally, but rarely seen, cougars.

Recently, a large cougar went on a killing spree at a

farm near the Bow River and killed six alpacas and two sheep in one night. That old tomcat weighed over two hundred pounds and was eventually shot by a neighbor after a few days of chaos. A young cougar was even spotted in Fish Creek Park last summer, right in the city and was hissing at the passing bird watchers and families out for a nature walk, while it devoured a young deer it had taken down.

Some naive and well-meaning people like to feed the deer in the park, leaving them apples and mixed birdseed. These well-fed, docile deer attract black bears and cougars. Concerned Conservation Officers closed the park to the public and attempted to live trap the cougar for a couple of days without success. With public pressure mounting, they brought in professionals with a pack of hounds. Remarkably, they had the young cat treed in less than an hour and safely relocated it.

The pelicans drift past and Dave returns to his casting. I step back from the water's edge and follow as he works his way upriver. Ten minutes of fishing pass, and then suddenly, there is a brief flash of yellow gold near his fly. The Brown Trout comes up for a look but quickly turns away, mere inches from the fly and disappears down into the watery ether to its dark lair. Dave drifts a couple of dozen more casts over the same spot hoping for a miracle, but hope can often mislead and keep you stuck in the same place.

My cell phone vibrates. It's Rich.

"Morning. How are you fella's making out?" he asks.

I walk away, out of earshot.

"Great, we're just working the water," I respond.

Then he teases, "Boy, the fishing was on fire this morning. My guys boated a dozen on big foam Stonefly drys. Two over twenty inches, a big Brown buck that taped twenty-one inches and a nice Rainbow around twenty. It slowed down about an hour ago, so we switched to the nymphs, but the fish have shut down now. You guys should have gotten out bright and early like we did. We launched my drifter at Policeman's Flats around 4:30 a.m.—"

I bite my tongue and say nothing.

"Hold on. I gotta go. Dave's just hooked a monster Brown. Wow, it has to be at least twenty-five inches," I exclaimed excitedly and hung up promptly before Rich could reply. I let out a little chuckle.

Dave pauses and takes a drink from his bottle of water as I walk back over to him. "See any more fish move to the fly?" I enquire.

"Nothing," he says with a headshake. The wind shifts to the south and intensifies. Well, at least it's blowing upstream I tell myself. "Maybe we should add a Caddis pupa as a dropper fly," I suggest. "It's almost noon so there should be a few Caddis starting to emerge " I tell him.

"Okay, let's try that" Dave agrees.

I tie a Caddis pupa on to an 18-inch section of fluro tippet and attach it to the hook bend of the Stonefly. "This should get the job done" I tell him confidently. "And let it swing out at the end of the drift like a natural emerger would," I instructed him.

Dave works the two-fly rig through the riffles near the head of the pool. A few casts and then a flash of silver. His leader slices the water as the Rainbow races out to the middle of the river and with a mighty leap and a few head shakes, it spits the dropper fly. Dave turns and looks at me with a grin so wide that his hat almost fell off. Game on!

Now my angler has become a hunter. He resumes fishing, leaning forward into each cast and creeping stealthily like a great blue heron stalking its dinner. Then, I hear it. Faintly, off in the distance, racing through the trees. Oh no, here it comes! Damn. The wind moves in from the south-west, growing louder and louder until it hits the water on the opposite shore, making little whitecaps as it pushes upstream against the current and crosses the river.

Dave stumbles and reaches up to hang onto his hat to keep it from being blown off his head. The air temperature has risen a few degrees in only a matter of minutes. It's the kind of wind that continually blows and pushes, only to be interrupted by even stronger gusts. It's tough on every angler. Dave is no exception. He struggles to make each cast and quickly tangles his flies. I suggest that we take a break and have a shore lunch. Maybe the wind will settle down in a while. There was still plenty of day left for optimism, but it was getting blown away, fast.

I had learned a lot about fly fishing and guiding from the late Gord Kennedy who had owned and operated WestWinds Fly Shop in Calgary for many years. I had spent a lot of time leaning on his front counter talking fly fishing with him. Gord taught me that the most important thing to being a successful guide was to try and make sure that the client had a great day. He would say, "The fishing isn't always going to be fantastic; the client isn't always going to be a skilled angler and the weather will rarely be perfect. Yes, you needed to know how to read the water, the river conditions, know the hatches and all the fly-fishing methods and tactics but, equally important, is how to read the client." Words of wisdom.

It was Alberta Badlands hot under the high noon sun, so we moved into the shade of the tree canopy to have our lunch.

"Why the old fishing creel?" Dave inquires.

"It was my dad's," I reply. "I've been fishing with it since I was nine. He won it in a raffle with a Mitchell 300 spin caster rod and reel, at a Hardware store in a small town where I grew up. He always let me use it and I never fish without it. It reminds me of the years that I spent fishing with him. I'm a lucky man to have had a father like him, Dave. He took me fishing when I was four years old, and I caught two small brookies. I've been hooked ever since."

Dave shares a few details of his life story and fishing experiences with his family down in California. Our conversation flows easily for three quarters of an hour, moving effortlessly from one question to another, from fishing to psychology, which he tells me was the first degree he completed before going into medicine. Not surprising for a typical Alma overachiever. But Dave has zero ego and is more interested in my story, always finding common ground when relating his experiences with mine.

I recall my aunt asking me when I was seven years old what I wanted to be when I grew up and I said, "a brain surgeon," because grown-ups seemed pleased with that answer. I wonder if Dave said that when he was seven? I wonder what Dave really wanted to be when he grew up? I forgot to ask him; I usually ask everyone that. When I was seven, I already knew what I wanted to be—a musician. I already was one at seven. I have been a musician for as long as I can remember. My mother and grandmother were teaching me to sing while I learned to talk and how to play simple nursery rhyme melodies on the piano before I could even read or write. I'm very lucky to have had such a caring mother and grandmother as I did. I don't remember ever not being a musician in my life... Ever. So that's what I did when I grew up. And what an adventure that is.

"Well, are you ready to throw some more tailing loops?" I tease with a grin.

"Let's give it another try," Dave says with a smile.

The wind remains unrelenting. Dave tries his best side arm cast to get the fly out to the current seam, but the cross wind is ferocious and blows his line back towards the shore. His leader tangles on about every third cast and in frustration, he starts trying to muscle the casting, making things even worse.

After fifteen minutes of struggle, Dave turns to me and with a look of defeat and says, "That's enough for today." He looks exhausted. We collect our things and head for refuge from the sun and gale. "I'm feeling a bit of jet lag today and this wind has just finished me off," he says when we get in the car.

"Yes, these conditions are impossible" I console. "The afternoon is still young though; would you like a quick tour around Calgary to see the sights?" I ask. "I'm still on the clock," I add.

"Sure, that sounds great," he replies.

We drive back into the city and up the hill to the Lookout in Crescent Heights, for a spectacular view overlooking downtown Calgary. Dave is impressed with how new, clean and beautiful Calgary's downtown office towers look next to the bottle green ribbon of the Bow River. Then I drive over to Kensington to show him its many small sidewalk boutiques, cafés, and restaurants. All of the patios are full of patrons and the festive spirit, smell and sounds of Stampede fills the street.

Dave tells me that Calgary reminds him of Seattle, clean, young and vibrant. He is amazed at the multicultural diversity here in Canada and how it seems so normal. I offer to take him up to the observation deck of the Calgary Tower for a Panoramic view of the city and the Rocky Mountains, but he declines, with thanks. He's tired and wants to have a short nap before supper, so we head back to Hotel Alma.

We unload his things at the lobby doors and Dave says, "That was great, Greg, I had a fantastic day, thank you." He reaches into his pocket and pulls out his wallet. He hands me his business card and a crisp, new $100 US bill and says, "Let me know if you are ever in California. I'll take you out and show you all my favorite fishing spots."

"I would certainly love to take you up on that offer, Dave, thank you. It was a pleasure spending the day with you." I shake his hand and leave, thinking that if Dave lived in Calgary, we would probably be fishing buddies. I drive a short distance and park to check my phone.

It's likely that my kids have sent me a dozen messages by now. We are very close; it's been ten years since their mom passed. I've had a very busy life raising our two boys, who are now in their late teens. Some wounds never heal...ever.

My phone vibrates; it's Rich calling, "Are you fellas still fishing?" he inquires.

"No, Dave had enough for the day. I just dropped him off."

"Yeah, we quit early too. We packed it in at noon when the wind picked up. Listen, John and Bill from Portland, Maine are back up here fishing with me this week. They're sitting here in the garage lounge with me having a glass of Scotch, I'm on speaker phone."

"Hi Greg" John and Bill say.

"Hi guys, welcome back to Calgary," I reply.

"So, they want you to take them out for another evening dry fly hunt, like you did last year," Rich continues.

"Sure, that sounds great, we had a lot of fun" I tell

them. John is a lawyer, originally from New York and Bill is a chartered accountant who grew up in Bangor, Maine.

"Okay then, pick them up here at the house tomorrow evening at 6:00 pm. Oh, by the way, did Dave land that big Brown that he hooked this morning?" Rich asks.

"Of course"... I lie.

Greg Allard lives and plays in Calgary, Alberta. He is currently busy teaching his two seven-year-old grandkids how to fish. He can be found most weekdays during the fishing season, sitting on the banks of the Bow River contemplating ideas for his first book, "Trout Fishing and Other Great Mysteries of the Universe."

TEN

A LOVE STORY

David McCumber

O N A sweet June day, I fell in love with Montana. It's a short flight from San Francisco to Missoula, two and a half hours give or take the caprice of the jet stream as it too visits the Rockies in the summertime, which it does more frequently now than when I made that flight in 1987—part of the not-so-slow-motion horror we call climate change. Shy of the contraption Jeff Goldblum shared with a horsefly, there are few quicker trips into an alternate life. I was almost instantly besotted, and my personal path was changed forever.

In Missoula's then-one-horse airport, I rented a car and headed toward a cabin on the West Fork of the Bitterroot. An early-sixties Ford F100 appeared in front of me, headed south out of Florence, and I was thoroughly charmed by it—the faded blue paint that matched the checkered shirt of the slim, straight-backed, Stetson-clad driver, a weathered, knobby hand gripping the top of the open window frame, his equally silver-haired sweetie sitting hip to hip with him on the left side of the cab.

As I followed them, I wondered whether their entire lives had been spent in that perfect little glacier-carved valley. Where were they headed that day? Going to change the dams in an emerald-green hayfield, in the magical space between the Sapphire and Bitterroot ranges, under that perfect unbroken deep-blue sky? Or maybe off to a roadhouse for steaks and a dance to live music—a blue denim couple, gliding buckle to buckle, as Jerry Jeff Walker wrote: *We love a Bob Wills ditty*—or maybe one by Conway Twitty—"Mama, you look so pretty, wrapped up in Daddy's arms."

It was more than thirty years ago, and Mama and Daddy are almost certainly gone, now. If they are still in the valley, I wonder what they would think of it, and of the state, today.

Home prices have doubled since the plague years began, and are probably ten times what they were when that F100 tootled down Highway 93. Lear jets and helicopters jostle for airspace, bringing in landowners for weekend visits. Much of the state, including the Bitterroot, is astronomically expensive and exponentially crowded, compared to that placid day that changed my life.

That day in 1987, of course, just got better and better. Falling in love is like that. Stopping at a gas station in Darby, I saw a cardboard displaying someone's home-tied flies by the cash register. "Stimulators $1.50," the sign said, and the big size 8 orange bugs looked good enough to eat, so I bought the remaining four on the card. Fly-tying legend Randall Kaufmann must have had a disciple in Darby. An hour later, in the velvet of near-twilight, I tied one on and flipped it into a riffle on the tiny upper West Fork, about twenty feet from where I stood in the knee-high snowmelt.

I've relived that moment so many times. It was like encountering a Peterbilt on a bike path, but much more pleasant. I suppose the stimmie was taken for a grasshopper, or possibly a stonefly, but either way, the brook trout bought into the concept enthusiastically. I was stunned at the vicious take and the bend in my little 4-weight, and when I had that fat fish in my hand, seventeen glistening inches, spotted green and red and mystical, my Montana seduction was complete. I've caught bigger fish, but never one so unforgettable.

Within five years I had divorced, moved to Bozeman and started a magazine, *Big Sky Journal,* that celebrated the place I adored. So, I'm part of the problem. Of course, my love affair with Montana is not unusual; so many have fallen in the same love and moved in the same direction, and look where we are now. Indeed, the magazine I started has for a quarter-century helped to light the spark in others' eyes that still glows brightly in my own, and without my help it continues to do so very well to this day. I've helped prime the pump, encourage the gush of new arrivals.

There's plenty of blame to go around. "A River Runs Through It" came along in 1992, and suddenly real estate ads with that title were ubiquitous, along with "The Last Best Place," a phrase Bill Kittredge supposedly conjured mid-martini at Chico Hot Springs.

That description of Montana was certainly true when Kittredge and Annick Smith created the momentous literary anthology by that name in 1990. It might still be true, given the fact that the rest of the American West has similarly declined in quality of life in the ensuing two decades-plus; and, of course, the quality of life on both coasts has declined exponentially more.

So much has changed, and we are the poorer for it.

Chico, of course, was certainly a "best place" in those tranquil and magnificent eighties and nineties. I remember Mike Art sitting in the bar one gray winter afternoon, relating the story of his day: He had visited his Livingston banker to explain that the resort's laundry had suffered a catastrophic failure, and to request an advance to take care of it. When the banker's first response was that Mike was all borrowed up, he tossed his bulky key ring on the banker's desk and said, "Okay. You run the son of a bitch without clean sheets."

The banker quickly relented, and Mike's piece of Paradise ultimately prospered. Today, considerably gussied up and under the caring stewardship of Colin and Seabring Davis, it has somehow remained magical.

But what of the perfectly named valley that surrounds Chico, that cradles the mighty Yellowstone as it flows north from the Park, growing from its humble beginnings up near Younts Peak and the Two Ocean Plateau to become the longest undammed river in the lower 48? The Paradise Valley is one of those impossible-to-forget Montana places. Yes, there are many of those across our six hundred miles of beauty—hundreds of drainages, hundreds of mountain ranges, and a rolling infinity of prairie. How many of those unforgettable places imprinted upon our collective consciousness are being lived-in and loved to death?

In the Paradise Valley, as ranches are broken and sold, as improbable mansions and entire subdivisions spring up, as wheel lines and pivots spray the bottomlands, suddenly the Yellowstone's flows have become meager in the heat of the summer, fish have turned belly-up in alarming numbers, and solitude has become the valley's fastest-dwindling resource.

The next major drainage to the West is in similar straits. The great rush to Bozeman has brought so many enthusiastic fly fishers, mountain bikers and rafters that the Gallatin Valley between the glittering college town and the fast-growing resort town of Big Sky is a summertime spectacle of Sage and spandex.

When I make the drive up U.S. Route 191 through Gallatin Canyon these days and see one or two anglers plying each riffle and pool, I think of March 1993, when I set out every day to fish a different stretch of the river cannily named by Lewis & Clark for then-Secretary of the Treasury Abraham Alfonse Albert Gallatin.

From the Taylor Fork up in the park to the confluence that makes the Missouri, I reveled in that river. In the first week, dawn would find me slipping into the chill waters, throwing a meaty stonefly nymph with a tiny hare's ear on a dropper. I remember laughing out loud one unforgettable morning as blue-wing olives ignored a sudden snow flurry and hatched by the thousands at Gallatin Gateway, and rising fish suddenly dappled the river from bank to bank. By month's end I was fishing more in the late afternoons and evenings, and a few stoneflies and even some caddis were making appearances on top of the water between Manhattan and Logan.

Other than the few people who went with me, Greg Keeler and Tom Wesen among them, I saw exactly four other fishermen all month. One of them I saw twice, a solitary pipe-smoking gentleman standing in the shadows of Axtell Bridge, and the following day half a mile downstream.

It's not enough, of course, just to reflect on the past and bitch about the present. There is work to do, and there is still land and water to enjoy, and to conserve for others. We are lucky, today, for yesterday's efforts of Montanans like Tony Schoonen and Jim Goetz, both instrumental in making stream access settled law in the state, and for the courage of politicians who joined the fight for public-lands access and conservation.

But the facts on the ground, and on the river, can be discouraging. Look at the Madison, where persistent efforts to stop greed-based overfishing have failed, so far, to gain traction. Yet to the west, people like Guy Alsentzer, Wade Fellin, and Dean Peterson are fighting spiritedly and intelligently to prevent the magnificent Big Hole from falling victim to the deadly threats of crowding and development.

Alsentzer is the Upper Missouri Watershed's riverkeeper, and Fellin is a fishing outfitter and co-owner and manager of Big Hole Lodge with his father, Craig Fellin. Dean Peterson is a rancher in the upper Big Hole Valley. Peterson serves on the Big Hole Watershed Committee, an organization in which ranchers and conservationists work together for the good of the river. They don't always agree about what should be done, but Peterson, like his father, who was a founding member of the committee in 1995, knows one thing that everybody can agree on: If ranchers lose the ability to run cow-calf operations like his in the valley, and grow the hay that sustains them, they will be replaced by subdivisions that will change the face of the valley, just as they have in the Paradise Valley and elsewhere. So many elsewheres in Montana.

Craig Fellin was instrumental in starting the Big Hole River Foundation, which hopes to leverage the many affluent fly fishers and others who fall in love with the river and would like to conserve it. The Foundation, now under the leadership of executive director Brian Wheeler, has performed an essential function in recent years, doing the careful monitoring of water quality that is actually the state's responsibility—one the state says it doesn't have the resources to fulfill.

What they have found is not such good news. They have discovered nutrients in the water, likely from cow manure, aging septic systems and from fertilizers used by the big hay operations in the valley. The context for this discovery is particularly concerning. During the last legislative session, Montana's numeric standards for nutrients like phosphorous and nitrogen, which were applauded by conservationists when they were instituted in 2014, were abolished in favor of "narrative" standards.

Senate Bill 358, abolishing the numeric standards, was introduced by Sen. John Esp, Republican of Big Timber. The bill's backers said compliance with the standards was too expensive for discharge sources such as water treatment plants, while opponents said the "narrative" standards are subjective and ambiguous. Excessive nutrients cause harmful algal blooms in rivers. It will be fought out in court, but for the Big Hole, the only river in the lower 48 that is habitat for fluvial Arctic grayling, the stakes are particularly high. Even as the state lessens its oversight, the long-term answer is Montana citizens like Peterson, Alsenter and Fellin. When citizen concerns are followed by action, anything is possible, and seeing that work have good effect on what many call Montana's "Last Best River" is particularly gratifying and encouraging. Maybe the future is not simply a shit-rain of warming, heedlessness, and ruin.

For me, the love affair born on the West Bitterroot has spread far, to the Milk River in the far northeast corner of Montana, where a Glasgow High School student, during a talk I gave on writing, raised his hand in the back of the auditorium and asked, "What should we write about?"

"What do you love to do?" I answered. "Start out writing about that. I love to fish, and so I love to write about fishing."

"Well let's go fishing then," he said, to laughter, but after the assembly was over I hopped into his old Dodge pickup and we thumped and bumped over a field to the Milk, reduced by summer heat to something much smaller, and muddier, than what I had imagined. He had an extra spinning rod, and we threw metal lures into the cloudy, slow-moving water, and caught crappie and catfish, and talked about the importance of living your passions, and writing about them, and the simplicity of that warm afternoon on a muddy river bank, and the purity of his writing aspirations, made me love Montana all over again.

My love deepened during the year I worked on Bill Galt's ranch, on land I came to love far more profoundly than any other. It was land where we fed hay in January blizzards to cows, calves, yearlings, bulls and horses who needed us to survive; where we collected calves born in those blizzards before they froze to death—or at least we tried; where we pulled calves and also pulled porcupine quills out of protective mother cows' noses; where we irrigated the old-fashioned way, with canvas dams and sticks, and the new way, with big wheel lines and pivots; where we fought fire, and shoveled shit, and gathered renegade cows, and fixed fence in places so beautiful all I could do was gape open-mouthed at my surroundings.

When you spend a fall day walking up the side of a mountain to bring cows and calves to shorter fences, or, if you're lucky, go after them ahorseback; when you run bulls through a squeeze chute on a gray cold winter morning to disinfect their penises and vaccinate them, getting them primed to do their jobs come spring; when you resuscitate an old abandoned branding trap and turn it into something that will once again hold cattle; when you carve a fireline on the side of a hill, hacking at creeping juniper with a Pulaski as smoke from the coming blaze fills your lungs; when you wean calves from their moms on a late fall day and load them into a truck, knowing that some among them survived and thrived because of your care, you feel different about a place.

That place, that hundred thousand acres of pasture and forest and all that lies in between, that place where you were chased by moose, where you cleaned up after fence-busting elk, that place where coyotes can be heard somewhere close by in the purple twilight, becomes a part of you.

And if, burbling through the western end of that ground, is a spring creek that rises incongruously from the side of a scrubby hill in a pasture and runs twenty-five miles through the ranch, beneath great red cliffs and past a magnificent old ranch house and barn before emptying into the Smith River, you know that you have found your favorite place on this planet.

And in that place is my personal salvation.

When Montana in the early 2020s becomes particularly vexing, my lover turned into a cheap caricature of itself by forces I can't control or even understand, that creek is my retreat and my renewal. I walk its banks, sharing them with the occasional rabbit or rattlesnake, fishing the pools with a precious 3-weight, 6-foot bamboo rod made by the master Glenn Brackett that is perfect for brushy creeks, catching as many trout as I care to with a metronomically consistent pattern: Rainbow, rainbow, rainbow, Brown. Rainbow, rainbow, rainbow, Brown. Rainbow, rainbow, rainbow, Brown.

The rainbows are 10 to 12 inches as a rule. The Browns are a lot larger. Catch a couple, wait for 10 minutes by the hole, catch a couple more—or simply move to the next hole and repeat. There is no cell service. No fences, no wires, no garbage or anything else man-made. Just the loveliest country I will ever see, with a brand-new thrill waiting around every bend in the creek.

I will always love you, Montana.

ELEVEN

THERE'S THIS CANADIAN GUY

Chris Pibus

IT WAS LATE OCTOBER, the last week of the season at Big Hole Lodge, and we were about to start a float trip on the upper section of the river. Our guide Wade Fellin had the day planned out carefully, and the first order of business was to send me to some wadeable water while he coached my friend Peter on the art of casting a fly from the complex platform of a moving drift boat.

"Walk up about two hundred yards," Wade said, "Until you see a big willow on the opposite bank. There's a deep run where I've seen a good fish."

Earlier that morning at breakfast we had talked about the miraculous survival of fluvial Arctic grayling in the river, the only watershed supporting a native population in the contiguous United States. I wandered over to study the wooden plaque on the wall recording the roster of anglers who had achieved the Big Hole Grand Slam, landing all five species (including grayling) in a single day. The dates extended back to the 1980s when the lodge began operations. Some quiet years had a couple of entries; others had more. We spoke about the October Caddis hatch and I was anxious to try the big rust-colored dry fly that had taken up permanent residence in my box for at least twenty years— with no hookup that I could remember. Wade had shaken his head and told me to save it for the cutthroats on the Bitterroot.

"Try this," he said later at streamside, handing me a Purple Haze, parachute style, with a neon color scheme straight out of the psychedelic Sixties.

Don't second-guess your guide, I said to myself, especially one with his background. Between Wade and his father, Craig Fellin, they had spent more than fifty years covering every square foot of the Big Hole, everything from pool to rapid to what they memorably called dumps, as I was about to discover. So, I tied the fly on the tippet with a dutifully improved clinch knot.

Wade and Pete turned the drift boat downstream and headed for a pod of rising whitefish for practice. It was a shivery morning in the mid-40s Farenheit, bright and clear all the way up the valley beyond the town of Wisdom, the last vestige of the original name of the Big Hole itself, chosen by Lewis and Clark to honor the "selibrated (sic) character" of their patron, Thomas Jefferson. To the southwest the Pioneer mountains saw-toothed the horizon, frosted with snow along the edges of the peaks. We had the river to ourselves, a rare blessing on the Big Hole due to the lateness of our booking.

I found the destination pool, unmistakably crowned by a solitary willow. Although it was completely still, the air was populated with falling yellow leaves, carried off by the weight of a heavy dew. My hands were shaky as I dressed the fly with floatant and began to watch the foam line along the edge of the current. Farther upstream, something seemed to break the surface. There was no splash; it was almost imperceptible. Yet, unless I was dreaming, that was surely a nose and a deliberate unhurried eat.

It took a few false casts to reorient myself to the eight-foot Wes Jordan cane rod after spending the previous day throwing streamers with a big graphite rod. It was time to slow everything down. On the third cast I marked the white upright wing sweetly tracking down the foam line, until the smallest commotion broke the surface and the fly disappeared. I tightened and backed up fast out of the deeper pocket, never quite sure of the connection. A big golden-sided brown trout took off upstream, clearing the water in a low arc. I could hardly breathe.

The trout turned and came downstream in a flash, quickly building slack as I back-peddled in a floundering attempt to maintain pressure. And then it was gone. The fly had pulled out; my doubts about the hook up proved lamentably accurate or maybe they contributed to a self-fulfilling failure. But it was early yet, I told myself. The world lay all before me, as the great blind poet once wrote; it was still a beautiful morning and evidently the fish were on the fin.

I waded about forty yards upstream to the foot of some fast water. Tight to the bank a boulder was deflecting the flow, creating a deeper bucket. The moment the Purple Haze touched down it was engulfed and obliterated in a thrashing administered by another good-sized brown. It was one of the angriest takes I have ever witnessed in fifty years of fly fishing, instantly snapping the tippet. Seems I was trespassing in a no-fly zone or just maybe the trout was not a Jimi Hendrix fan.

I wandered down the river to find my companions and to thank Wade for putting me onto some fine fish. He looked up at me gravely and I could see him thinking you only get so many chances on this river. But all he said was, "It's time to change up your rig."

For Wade Fellin, like his father, the Big Hole watershed is sacred territory, whose welfare commands his earnest attention. Wade is a true river keeper in all its complex contemporary dimensions. Alongside his day-to-day responsibilities for lodge operations, he guides throughout the summer and stays fully engaged in the politicized world of riparian rights management all over southwestern Montana. Since 2013 he has worked for Upper Missouri Waterkeeper, first as a founding member and now as Program Director and attorney, managing their enforcement initiatives against polluters. At first glance he looks younger than his years, but he is a committed and purposeful man in everything he does, as I learned that morning on the river. As a guide he is serious about results; I saw it in his eyes as he absorbed the story of my mishaps, unforgivingly dark under black brows.

Handing over the nine-foot Sage rod, with two caddis nymphs in tandem, he told me to walk downstream about a half-mile, tracing the edge of the pasture.

"You'll find a big pool, start at the tail and work your way up. Most of the risers will be whitefish but there are big trout where the river dumps in at the head."

A rail fence ran along the bank towards a small butte that marked the location of the pool. I paused to look upriver and saw that Wade had anchored the boat midstream and positioned Pete in the bow casting an indicator rig and slowly working out some line. Between casts, Pete kept looking up at two circling eagles, even as the guide yelled "SET" and directed his attention back to the currents, the bobber, and the possibility of a whitefish.

Pete and I had become friends at high school in Montreal, where his talents as a cross-country runner first emerged. We lost touch when he left for Duke University on a track scholarship but met up again later at school in Toronto. Pete went on to become a world-class long-distance runner, competing in marathons around the world including Fukuoka in Japan and the world Championships in Helsinki in the early 1980s. In October 1982, he won the Toronto Marathon— the biggest Canadian race of its kind. I promised to be there at Varsity Stadium for the final lap but lamentably missed him crossing the finish line by ten minutes.

And now, after more than forty years of friendship, this was not only our first serious fishing trip, but Pete's first experience with a fly rod, though he had heard all about my obsessive connection to the sport. We had flown into Bozeman on separate flights from Toronto and Cincinnati and as usual Pete expressed no surprise when I appeared an hour late.

I was delighted to find him at the luggage carousel, flourishing a rod case like half the other travelers at the airport. In his sixties, he remained remarkably fit, retaining the lean physique of an elite runner. His boyish features and perpetually bright eyes projected a sense of openness that he has never lost. Although he practiced as an attorney for more than thirty years, and was a resolutely competitive athlete, he is the least predatory person I have ever met. He has always been a steadfast, patient, and unfailingly amiable man, despite health setbacks over the years and the peaks and valleys of remission and recurrence.

I reached the big pool and walked down to the tail mesmerized by the sight of dozens of rising fish, as Wade had predicted. Overlapping rise forms carpeted the surface, the rings multiplying before my eyes. I worked my way up, hooking a couple of whitefish and keeping my eye on the drift boat's slow progress down the river. Wade and Pete pulled into shore above the pool as I stood studying the currents. There was a short shallow run of rapids at the head, and then the river turned over on itself along a ledge where the fast water was swallowed up into the depths.

"Your cast needs to be six feet above the shelf so the flies will be well down when they go over the dump. The fish will be sitting right there," Wade said pointing to the top of the flat water. "Sometimes you see their noses just where the dark water starts."

The two caddis nymphs landed short, barely catching the last foot of fast water but then shooting over the edge and out of sight, while Wade yelled "SET." This was a heavy fish, another brown judging by the deep yellow flank we could see as it turned. After a determined run into deep water, the hook pulled out.

Wade said nothing this time, just motioned me forward so the next cast could reach the second current seam. On the third try, finally, the nymphs landed well upstream and bumped smoothly over the shelf and into the depths. When the float moved sideways I struck hard, and my timing was good but overzealous as I broke the fish off. We never saw that trout, but to my mind it was surely another brown, dominant enough to command the prime feeding station in the pool.

Now I admit to having a proclivity for losing things that

goes back to childhood: everything from my first St. Christopher's medal to my first bamboo fly rod. And of course, I frequently lost track of time. But this was a new dimension of purgatory and loss, this was a cliff diver's descent into the Slough of Despond. I sat down hard on the bank and squeezed my eyes shut, vaguely aware of someone talking over the sound of the water.

It was Pete, shaking his head in sympathy, extending a hand to hoist me up while wondering about my abject state of devastation. "Well Christopher," he said, "Looks like there's a canyon up ahead so haul yourself into the boat and I'll show you how to do this properly."

I settled into the stern seat for some respite and began paying attention to Pete's intermittent casting. He wasn't distracted by the surroundings, he was absorbing it all in a state of wonder, seeing everything I would typically miss with my gaze fixed on the two-foot radius of surface and depth around my fly. Whenever he could, he was looking up and around at the achingly clear sky, the alternating stretches of riverside pasture and cottonwood thickets and now the steep-sided canyon that brought us into the shadows and cooler air.

Perched on a ledge near the top of the cliff-face, two bald eagles were watching our progress. A moment later they were soaring in unison, riding the thermals, and bound for heaven's gate.

I turned my focus back to Pete's indicator and began musing about the many days, following a long float trip, when I could recall like graven images the current seams and riffles where I had hooked or raised fish but had no memory of where exactly I was on the river. There were no maps or signposts, just a series of successive targets, flowing one into the other. Even my dreams were obsessive, full of moving water but oddly disembodied from the land-scapes that contained and released it.

The boat took us out of the first canyon to another pas-tured bank, with a single cottonwood standing sentinel at streamside. We could see a big nest, likely from the prior spring, sturdily wedged and anchored in a fork below the topmost branches. Wade spun the boat to the shore so Pete could get out and take a closer look. "Osprey?" I asked, thinking of the nests that had reappeared in recent years along the Bow River near Calgary. Wade pointed up, just as we heard the piercing whistle of the eagle overhead. The two birds had followed us downstream and began to circle high above the tree, in perfect synchronicity, then descending rapidly to mark our encroachment. One sud-denly broke out of the formation and swept straight up, pinions straining. We summonsed Pete back to the drift boat, and he scrambled over the side as the distinctive shadow of the circling bird crossed our path.

When we reached the next canyon, Pete's indicator slid sideways across a pocket. "Hit it," yelled Wade, and so we began fishing in earnest once again. Over the next four hours the fishing was steady, as the sun raised the water temperature and the change in fortune raised my spirits. We landed numerous good rainbows, two cutthroats and finally a ten-inch brook trout. In a stretch of fast water and rapid-fire casting, we each caught a lovely grayling, fitted out with its distinctive oversized dorsal fin —a silvery and purple-hued survivor from a golden age, still thriving in its Big Hole sanctuary.

It turned into a fine day, but as we approached the bridge and boat ramp, I could see that Wade had some-thing on his mind. "The Grand Slam," he said to me, "You've almost caught all five of them. Plenty of rainbows, a brookie, grayling, and even the toughest get of all—the cutthroat."

I thought back to the plaque hanging in the lodge and to the variety of grand slams I had heard about over the years, depending on the river and different resident populations. The inclusion of grayling and cutthroats on the list meant this was a challenge uniquely conceived and reserved for the Big Hole, a feat worthy of a great western river.

"All you're missing..." Wade began.

"I know, I know," I said, "All I'm missing are the browns I buggered up this morning."

"It's strange," he replied, "the river has plenty of brown trout —it's the other ones, especially the cutts that are hard to find."

Mulling it over, we realized we had not even glimpsed one since the late morning.

"Maybe the trout have been talking among themselves," I said.

"There's this Canadian guy," they're murmuring, *"who messed with four of our golden brothers this morning. We've given him every chance, but enough is enough."*

At the take-out, Wade directed me back to the big pool below the bridge and told me to cover all the likely seams with a caddis, while he drove Pete back to the lodge to join the group for supper. The two of us would stop at the Wise River Club and, once it was dark, we would try a pool where he'd had success night fishing for browns.

At the bar an hour later, Wade showed me photos on his phone, prodigious predatory night-caught browns, gleaming and brilliant in the flash surrounded by blackness. Thomas McGuane fished the Big Hole many times with Craig Fellin and wrote a fine chapter in The Longest

Silence paying tribute to the river in all its glory— but he never mentioned black ops fishing like this.

The night was clear and calm, the skinny moon low on the horizon. "You want the real darkness," said Wade as he scrambled down a gravel slope to the river and I picked my way gingerly after him. He had rigged up short heavy tippets with weighted streamers tied with deer hair heads thick enough to move water on the retrieve.

We measured out a twenty-foot cast and I punched the big streamer again and again into the void, sensing the surface of the river only by the pressure on my waders. We didn't hook any fish. I was busy trying to find a foothold on a slippery, unseen planet. Then I looked up — for the first time— at the vault of heaven, with the Milky Way saturating half the sky with great swaths of starlight. The world began spinning and I drifted downstream until Wade gripped my arm and pulled me back into the shallows, landed and duly released.

Next morning I was up long before breakfast, with a plan for early fishing on the Wise River where it runs through the lodge property, a few miles above its junction with the Big Hole itself. From our cabin it was a five-minute dew-sweeping hike through the pasture. There was one pool, with some good depth even in late October, tucked under a small trestle for irrigation water. I was hunting for brown trout, maybe a fall migrant from the big river. The early morning fly of choice was a Purple Haze. Below the riffle, at the head of the pool, I found a lovely twelve-inch brown in a taking mood— to borrow a phrase from George La Branche. A quick photograph to show Pete, and then I scrambled up the bank and out to the edge of the thicket.

Something was moving at the far end of the pasture, beyond the fence. Two massive antlers emerged from the long grass, and then a moose soared over the rails with astonishing grace, its front legs folded together in an attitude of prayer. Halfway across the field, it paused and slowly swung its great head in my direction, before continuing on its way in the baptismal light of a pure Montana morning.

∝

Chris Pibus grew up near the shores of the St. Lawrence River in Quebec and has been inspired and sustained by moving waters ever since. He is a writer and retired lawyer now living in Dundas, Ontario. Chris has been a fly fisherman for more than 50 years, and he loves the great rivers of Alberta and Montana, especially the Waterton and the Big Hole."

TWELVE

༄

THE TOTAL FISHING EXPERIENCE

Story and Recipes by Larry Kapustka
Photos by Mike Forbister.

Line to Table

Recipes

Shore Lunch

Trout Almondine

Lavender Infused Sturgeon, Halibut,
Cod, or Lake Whitefish

༄

PHOTO: MIKE FORBISTER

LINE TO TABLE
CAPTURING THE TOTAL
FISHING EXPERIENCE

Larry Kapustka

"All water has a perfect memory and is forever
trying to get back to where it was."
—Toni Morrison

*Author's note: I have only had the privilege of spending one short
afternoon on the Big Hole (a.k.a. Wisdom River) and it was special.
Three different hatches over two hours and each readily matched
with the proper fly. Indeed, a magical place. But so are so many
other rivers.*

WATER IS ever-changing as it flows. It passes by on
its journey to the sea, full of life, full of promise.
Without it, life shrivels, then dies. It is so for all beings,
microbes, plants, and animals.

Land animals know pleasure of finding clean, cool
water to drink, to modulate temperature, or provide nutritious food. In that regard, we humans are the same. But
we are different from others by virtue of our use of fire and
imagination.

Soon after reaching toddler stage, I began my journey
of life connected to water in creeks, rivers, lakes, and much
later, oceans. This is a journey of awe and inspiration, of
pleasure and humility, of sustenance and sharing.

At age three, in farm ponds and gravel pits in Nebraska,
I caught bluegills using a cane pole, a length of line equipped

with a worm on a hook and a red and white bobber. Around age six, I was gifted a cheap flyrod that launched me into the use of poppers, elevating the excitement of bites on the surface, punctuated by an occasional largemouth bass blowing a hole in the lake. These were family activities, in which my dad and older siblings fanned out across the lake or along a nearby river, leaving me with my mom (who seemed to get the largest bass on most outings).

Being on a farm, we tended to head out fishing on most Sundays from April through October. And though we reveled in the joy of catching a mess of fish, it was also an important source of food. We would clean our catch (scale, remove the head, tail, fins, and entrails – never skinning or filleting), salt them, and have a late-night dinner of fried fish and a few meals later in the week. These became foundational, cultural connections for me—line-to-table experiences.

The beginning of this journey included lessons on "reading the water," learning how to think like a fish. Were I a fish, where would I hang out so that there was plenty to eat and be protected from predators? Understanding the habits of each species, how those habits shift during the day, season, or weather event became second nature to me. Which structures, deadfalls, water plants, ledges are attractive? How far might a fish stray from the structure to grab a bite? All of this dictated the gear and skill set needed for success. Placement of the bait or lure had to be precise for maximum likelihood of getting a strike. By age ten, I was ready to compete with my dad, uncles, and brothers—we were formidable anglers.

I was in my mid-20s before I lived in trout country, and in my late 20s when I succumbed to the debased lifestyle of tying my own flies. My approach was not one in search of aesthetic perfection, but more along the lines of "is it good enough to fool an unsuspecting trout?" The first trout I caught on a fly I tied was memorable for many reasons. I had driven an hour plus for a few moments of fishing before dark. A beautiful 20-inch brown gobbled my fly. I decided that the one fish was good enough for the day. My Mother was visiting at the time and when I walked into the house proudly holding my catch, she remarked, "Is that all you caught?" I refused to let that dampen my joy.

Through the years, much has changed regarding fishing. Barbless hooks and catch-and-release are now the norm. Gone are the days of bringing home a mess of fish; indeed, not even one. This, at least for me, dampens the enthusiasm for spending a day on the water. I have a sense of guilt of hooking multiple fish that I know will have to be released. How is this not sadistic torture? Will the fish survive? It is for me easier to justify hooking a few or many in search of a keeper to bring home. Because only then can there be closure of preparing a wonderful meal to share with family and friends.

I understand the need for catch limits, including limits of zero. While fishable streams and lakes have remained the same or slightly diminished, the numbers of fisherpersons have grown exponentially over the past few decades. Gear has improved so that a skilled angler has few excuses. And collectively this places inordinate pressure on fragile fish populations. There are no good solutions. Even so, I cling to days gone by—and sharing a meal of fresh fish with special guests.

The full experience begins with the ritual of checking and rechecking rod, reel, line, and supply of tippets. Are the guides clean? Is the drag set properly. Do I have the best flies for the stream, for the season, for the weather? Have the barbs all been pinched? Is the truck gassed up? Tires and spare inflated? Waders, wading boots, vest, life jacket – check, check, check, check. What are the regs this year? This "pre-flight checklist" might be reviewed several times while the snow is still drifting, but it will be checked one last time the evening before.

Once on the water everything takes on a new sensation. Layers of the storied memory begin to materialize from a myriad of possibilities. It might be the majestic mating flight of a pair of bald eagles screaming high above, or the mysterious American dipper (a.k.a. water ouzel) walking on the bottom of a riffle picking off caddis fly larvae. On a rare occasion, a shadowy form slides through the water to emerge on the shore—the magnificent, playful river otter. As is the case when perched in a hunting stand, the depth of the experience is marked by the unexpected appearance of any number of birds and mammals. Or it might be the refreshing smell of bruised mint plants along the shore.

A hatch begins. Silvery flashes at depth expose feeding trout. Along a drift line, dorsal fins cut through the current punctuated by faint sounds of slurping. A frenzied few moments elapse while trying to find the fly that matches the emerging adult insects—which of the three species are the trout locked in on? And then all is quiet. That opportunity has passed without a hook-up. But the day is long, there will be something later.

Commotion along the overhanging sedge mat signals a new chance. Easing into position, measuring the length of the cast, waiting for the interval between rises—it is time. A gentle cast places the low riding salmon fly (a type of stonefly) a couple meters above the spot of the last two rises, a mere centimeter or two from the overhanging sedges.

The timing and placement were spot on. The fly drifts into the feeding window resulting in a slurping swirl. Hook set, the fight is on — a strong run downstream, a jump, a run upstream, another jump. She tires, slides into the landing net, and with a headshake tosses the fly. A beaut, unharmed save for a small sting in the lip, she slides out of the net and retreats to the depth of the pool.

Over the next two hours, the big fish continue to take the salmon fly. And then one sucks the fly deep into its gills resulting in a stream of blood sliding along its flanks. This one will go home with me. On shore, a quick blow to the skull plate ends its life. I pack up and head home.

A couple of days later, friends are invited to dinner. The trout, with only the gills and guts removed, is encrusted in a blend of sweated diced onion, chopped parsley, crushed toasted almonds, and lightly seasoned with lemon juice, salt, and fresh ground black pepper. The cavity is filled with the same mix. This will go on a soaked cedar plank ready for the grill as the guests arrive. It will be served with garden fresh green beans and a blend of whole grain and wild rice. An oaky chardonnay will complement the offering.

As the guests arrive, they are offered an assortment of cheeses, mixed nuts, and smoked mountain whitefish from an earlier excursion. The mood overall is joyous.

The appreciative guests take their places at the outdoor dining table that affords them a view of the Alberta Rockies as the sun sinks low in the sky creating accents of crimson, orange, and slate gray along puffy white clouds. Inevitably, questions about the catch are asked. I oblige with a narrative that need not be embellished as it is good enough as is. Together, we venture into ethics and philosophy, the gift of harvest, the exhilaration of being in a mostly natural setting. The authenticity that comes from eating from the bounty around us. I deflect the compliments stealing a sentiment I first heard expressed by the amazing chef Michael Smith of Prince Edward Island, "What makes it a great meal are the guests." But in my heart, I know what made it special were the water ouzel, the otter, the eagles, the fawn nosing the pool for a refreshing drink, unaware of my presence.

I have been privileged to learn how to prepare special meals, to build on what the French refer to as terroir. There is a special sense of place that comes with honoring the unique flavors imparted in the fish from the sediments they feed from. This is especially wonderful with a well-executed shore lunch. Sometimes all that is needed is a beautiful aromatic extra virgin olive oil, salt, and pepper and the fish on a grill or cast-iron skillet. Or one can go exotic as the time I infused fresh caught sturgeon with lavender blossom water so that it forecast the upcoming dessert of lavender crème brulee. In each meal, whether simple or exotic, the focus is to honor the fish to be eaten. Each time, it connects in some way to my childhood experiences; each time it presents the opportunity to relive the events from the winter-time pre-flight preparation through the catch, meal prep, and enjoyment. It, for me, is always a line-to-table moment.

SHORE LUNCH

There is something special that comes with the experience of a shoreline meal. It can be semi-elaborate or strikingly primitive.

INGREDIENTS

Freshly caught legal fish (filleted or steaked)
Cast iron frying skillet (lid optional)
Serving pan to hold cooked vegetables
Cooking oil
A Stick of Butter (1/4 cup)
Potatoes (one per person)
One large onion (white or yellow)
Carrots (one per person)
Can of Corn (or 1/2 ear per person)
One lemon
Salt
Coarse ground black pepper
One egg
For Options: coarse corn meal or batter

Premix flour, salt, pepper, baking soda and baking powder. *See instruction later for making a beer batter by stirring in an egg and beer.*

⌒〜

The first order of business is to catch the right-sized fish, not too big for your party and importantly, legal to harvest on the body of water you are fishing. On the primitive end of the spectrum, an unplanned lunch can provide a nice break. Start

cont...

a fire, remove the guts and gills of the fish, attach the cleaned fish to a stick of some sort (willow works well), and roast the fish over the open fire. Don't have a nice stick? Perhaps there is a flat-ish rock you can heat up and then lay the fish on. It's a bonus if you managed to have salt and pepper.

A more elaborate and memorable shore lunch involves advanced planning and a commitment to trade a bit more than an hour of fishing time to partake in a communal feast. The pre-planning part involves packing a cast iron skillet, a lid or foil, a slug of oil, a bag of premixed batter, butter, salt and pepper, potatoes, onions, corn, and if you are so inclined, a bottle of your favorite white wine (if permitted).

You can either do the deed yourself, but for a more rounded experience, divide the labor among everyone in the party. While someone is preparing the fish, others can be gathering fuel, building the fire, or cutting vegetables.

Prepare fillets or steaks of the fish (your choice depending on the size of the fish and your preference). Sprinkle salt and pepper on the fish and hold until the vegetables have been cooked.

Construct a fire ring, round up dry branches and kindling, and get a nice fire going. While the fire is building coals, cut the potatoes, carrots, onions, and corn—whatever you brought to be ready to put in a skillet when the fire dies down. When the coals are glowing, put a good splash of oil (about 1/4 cup) in the cast-iron skillet and place on the coals. Once the oil is hot, add the potatoes and carrots and cover. A splash of water added to the pan will speed cooking. Check that the potatoes are browning not burning, and when nearly done, add the onions, and corn; cover and cook for another five minutes or so until fork tender. Add salt and pepper to taste. Transfer from the skillet to a serving pan and cover to keep warm.

Cornmeal option—mix a couple of handfuls of coarse corn meal with salt and coarse-ground black pepper. After the vegetables have been transferred to the serving pan, add butter to the skillet and heat. Dredge the fillets or steaks in the seasoned corn meal and place these in the melted butter. Cooking time will depend on the thickness of the fillets or steaks. As above, avoid burning. When golden brown, turn the fish onto the other side and cook until done (flaky). Serve with a wedge of lemon if you thought to bring some, and the potato mix.

Beer Batter Option – Add beer (or water) and one egg to the prepared dry mix to achieve a consistency of pancake batter. Add enough oil to the skillet so that it is half inch deep. When the oil is hot but not smoking, dredge the fillets (or steaks) in the batter and carefully place in the oil (be careful to avoid splashing hot oil on yourself or onto the coals). When golden brown, turn and complete cooking. Serve with a wedge of lemon and the vegetable mix.

Enjoy!
Before leaving, douse the fire and double check that there are no remaining embers. And be damned sure to take all your trash with you!

PHOTO: MIKE FORBISTER

TROUT ALMONDINE

The basic shore lunch meals work at home but with a different ambiance. If you want to step it up a notch or two, and perhaps expose yourself to some derision from purist-friends, dress-up your trout with a gourmet preparation. A wild-caught trout in the range of 12 to 14 inch length will nicely serve four.

INGREDIENTS

One Trout (12 - 14 inches length), entrails and gills removed
Almond slivers (a handful)
Parsley (two bunches)
One large white onion
Rice (enough to serve four) – brown/wild rice mix
Butter (one stick, 1/4 lb.)
One lemon
Salt
Coarse ground black pepper

Remove the entrails and gills (leave the head on as the whole fish makes for a lovely presentation).

Toast the almond slices in a dry pan either on top the stove or in an oven. This requires careful attention to avoid burning the nuts. Spread the toasted slivers onto a large plate to cool. After the toasted nuts have cooled, finely chop about half of them; reserve the remainder as slices.

Finely dice one large white onion
Finely chop two bunches of parsley

Melt the stick of butter in a sauté pan. Sweat the
chopped onion in the melted butter. Add in the chopped
almond and parsley, salt, and pepper. Set aside to cool.
When cool enough to handle the mixture, fill the
trout cavity with some of the onion-parsley- almond mix
and mold the remainder around the trout. Decorate the
exterior with the toasted sliced almonds. Arrange the
trout on a cookie sheet or in a casserole pan, or similar
shallow-walled pan. Putting a slight bend in the fish;
flaring the pectoral fins will help stabilize the fish during
cooking. At this stage, the coated-stuffed trout can be
covered with foil and placed in a refrigerator until ready
to cook.

Preheat oven to 350 F (175 C). Place the pan with the fish in the oven for 35 to 45 minutes. When done the meat will separate from the spine easily; alternatively, one can check that the internal temperature is 150 F (63 to 65 C) with a meat thermometer. Arrange lemon wedges around the fish. Sprinkle the rest of the chopped parsley over and around the cooked fish.

Serve with your favourite rice (a mix of brown rice and wild rice is excellent) and a mixture of roasted vegetables, lemon slices and, if you are so inclined, a dry white wine.

Some guests like to have assistance with serving the fish. You can make a production out of it by peeling the flesh along the tail section on one side. And if it is cooked perfectly, the entire spine and rib cage bones will lift out in one piece and discarded. Be sure to extract the little morsels of cheeks from the head for a special treat.

LAVENDER INFUSED STURGEON/HALIBUT/LAKE WHITEFISH

INGREDIENTS

For this one, make it up!

 ⌒∞

This special meal emerged with a large dose of serendipity. The start was winning a bid for a sturgeon-fishing trip at a Rocky Mountain Elk Dinner in Oregon. There is a sturgeon run in early January that brings these prehistoric creatures up the Columbia River in pursuit of spawning smelt. Fishing near the confluence with the Willamette River, we were on sturgeon all afternoon. We were allowed one fish each in a certain slot size. Previously, I had enjoyed smoked sturgeon that my uncle Spud caught in the Missouri River while waiting for geese to decoy. I knew we were in for a treat.

After enjoying some of the sturgeon fresh, the rest were frozen to be enjoyed on special occasions. One gorgeous day in late May, our lavender bush was flowering. Susan announced that we would be having lavender crème brulee for dessert. It was up to me to prepare the rest of the festive repast. I decided to take a big risk with a package of sturgeon. I harvested a batch of lavender flowers from our garden and steeped the blossoms in hot water. When this had cooled, I submerged two sturgeon steaks into the fragrant tea and crossed my fingers in hope that I wasn't ruining this fine fish.

As evening approached, we made a fresh (hand made) pasta into which we substituted fresh crushed strawberries from our garden for some of the liquid. At mealtime, the pasta was cooked and dressed with a small amount of salted butter. Freshly picked home-grown snow peas were sautéed, and the lavender-infused sturgeon was pan-fried. A chilled bottle of oaky chardonnay from a favorite nearby winery comple-mented the flavors perfectly. The magic of the meal was realized when the dessert was served. The hint of lavender perfume from the sturgeon lingered as a bridge to the luscious crème brulee. That brought closure to an amazing experience.

Based on this experience, I am confident that some variation of this would work well with any firm white-meat fish (e.g., cod, halibut, lake whitefish). The hard ingredients to get in Alberta or Montana would be fresh lavender blossoms and beautifully ripe juicy garden strawberries. As with many foods, fresh from the garden ingredients; fresh from the waters elevate the flavors. A huge bonus is recalling the events of the catch, if you are so lucky. Instead of lavender blos-soms, try fruits of blueberries, cherries, or peaches when you are looking for a memorable dining adven-ture. And as you enjoy, you might reflect that it is unlikely that anyone, anywhere else is travelling the path you are on at that moment.

THIRTEEN

HIS RIVER TEACHINGS

Rayelynn Brandt

WATER FLOWS and everything changes. Water flows over, under, and through Earth's landscapes, carving jagged—edged mountainsides and shaping smooth, high valley refuges through millennia. The vast plains of Earth where water runs slowly are braided with deposition from the mountains, seeding the land with nutritious soil that feeds the planet's lifeforms. The deepest canyons are carved from the torrent of waters running each spring, making their transformation from ice to river to ocean, carrying with them the Earth's crust, moving it from mountain to coast. Water shapes all life on Earth, making itself essential and adapting all forms of life to its power. And so it is with us humans too. Water shapes us, defines us, inspires us, sustains us. Without it we die. What wisdom does water hold for us? What lessons are available to us as we reflect upon the awesome power and beauty of water and specifically, its movement?

Growing up in Montana, I think I knew what a watershed was in the same way that a fish understands water. I didn't have vocabulary or description for my home other than it just is. Much the same as I assume fish know water—just as it is—I knew that water moves from the mountains to the rivers as readily as I knew my own name. So, how was this knowledge imparted to me? How did the understanding that snow on the mountains in July signified plentiful fishing throughout the summer become etched in my mind? How was it that I knew the scientists were right about climate change and the dangers to Earth's water resources when I was only in middle school, well before Al Gore's movie, "An Inconvenient Truth?" It had to be that the river itself taught me these lessons, using my greatest teacher—my dad—as naturalist and guide.

My earliest memories of my father flash into my mind. I am seated in a backpack, bouncing along a mountain trail and I hear his voice yelling to our Chesapeake Bay retriever, with a joyous singsong, "Get out of the water!" Dad is laughing and my dog is bounding with happiness. My memory is not clear, but rather a collection of colors and the feeling of joy rising in my belly. I smile to myself as I think back to how many miles he must have trudged with me strapped to his back. We have photos of us during these days and he relays the stories of the high mountain lakes we visited, father, daughter, and dog. My mother laughs that she always stayed below in the campgrounds while he hiked with me for miles. According to them, I never complained or cried while in the backpack: but, had he tried to go without me, there would be a wailing to chill the bones of the dead. The water was calling to me even at this early age.

Water has an energy to it, its power and might niggles at my ankles when I step into the river. Dad always reminds me to be careful and respectful of the river as its energy can sweep me downstream in a heartbeat. I find that I am renewed by this energy, that the moment I step into the river, my worries and cares also wash downstream. I feel the gentle sway of the river against my legs and, as I hang my hand into the water before I load the fly rod for the first cast, suddenly my heart lifts and I have forgotten the fatigue of the day.

The morning my father died, I was shocked and speechless. I found him in his kitchen, the giant hulk of a man lifeless on his floor, taken by a heart attack. My rock, my protector, the one whose wisdom and teaching I relied upon for all of my days was gone. Who would show me the ways of life? Who was my mentor and teacher now? I sobbed on his chest as I waited for the funeral home personnel to come take his body and at one point I laughed out loud, with tears streaming down my face. Strange how inappropriate humor strikes in times of great angst. I was laughing because when I was little, I was certain that his life would be taken by the river. My mind was flooding with memories of lessons he taught me about how water gives us life, but it also takes and that I needed to be careful, to honor water and to respect its power and energy.

Before he learned the art of fly fishing, my dad had a little aluminum boat, with an outboard motor barely large enough to carry himself, a friend, and me. Each spring, he would run the motor in a fifty-gallon drum to ensure that all things mechanical were tuned and humming along correctly. I would watch this process with fascination. This annual ritual was typical of most things in his life. He was careful and deliberate with planning and took the time to be certain he was ready for what lay ahead.

"Why do you do that, Dad? With the motor?"

"When we get out to the lake, that would be the worst time to find out our motor doesn't run. Or worse yet, it quits running when we are in the middle of the lake." His voice is stern and I hear the importance of his words. I look up into his eyes intently as he continues.

"You see, when you are on the water, you have to remember that the lake can be dangerous if you are not careful. It's fun to be out and it's usually safe, but the one time you don't maintain things, is the time that you will regret. Just as water gives us life, it can take it too. Remember that."

As a little girl, I learned to swim early. Dad always made sure that we both had our life jackets whenever we were in the water. He would joke and cajole that he wasn't a good swimmer, so if the boat tipped, I was to swim for the shore and let him sink. His joking scared me. What would I do without my father? This man was my life when I was a child.

As we started wading and floating rivers together, he taught me the important lessons of wearing my wading belt, using a wading staff, being aware of my surroundings, and pulling my knees to my chest and relaxing if I fell. "Just float through and you will find a spot where you can stand up, be calm and you will be okay." I was older now, bigger, stronger and a confident swimmer. He still did not like to swim, but at 6'5" I felt assured that there weren't many places he would get into trouble wading. He would often playfully tease me, remarking that if he were to fall into the river, I should let him go, as he might pull me under with him. I hated those words. While his advice held wisdom in terms of safety, the mere thought of letting go of my father was inconceivable to me. Letting him go was out of the question in my mind. I filed away the lessons along with the fear that he would fall and drown and I would be powerless to help him. My mind jumps back into the present, and here I sit on the kitchen floor, letting him go. The river did not take him.

∽

Our favorite rivers were the ones outside of our watershed. Our watershed's river, the Clark Fork and its tributary creeks of Blacktail and Silver Bow, were examples of death in my father's teachings. We'd drive by Silver Bow Creek on our way to make the exit to the road that brought us to the Big Hole River and dad would point out the window, telling me that creek has been dead a long time: that there were no fish there.

"What happened to the creek? Why is it dead?"

"Progress."

One simple, short word ringing in my ears. Progress. What does that mean? My mind is reaching for the next question as I recognize this as an opportunity to show off what I know about things. He smiles and waits.

"You mean the creek is dead because of people building out here and using the water?"

"Yes. But more than that, sweetheart. It is dead from greed."

Again, my mind reaches for what he means. Were the people taking too much water? Was the creek used up somehow? I look at the sandy yellow beaches along the creek banks. These beaches are not found along the other creeks where we wade and fish. There are no trees lining the creek, which would make it easier for me to cast my line as I wouldn't be constantly snagged, but that isn't the same as our favorite river at all. I keep peering out the window, knowing that he wants me to think, to observe, to consider what else I am seeing out my window as we drive by.

"Is it polluted? Is that why it's dead?"

"Yes, honey. The mines polluted our rivers here. It's why we drive over the Divide to fish." The tenor of his voice lilts with the sadness I had come to recognize when he felt a sense of injustice.

"Why did they pollute it? Is that what the yellow beaches are? Pollution?"

"Exactly right. Those are tailings, which come from mining. As to why they polluted it, well, I think they would say that they didn't know any better and I suppose that is true for the average miner, but as for The Company, well, I don't give them as much of a pass."

The "Company" he was referring to was the Anaconda Company, but to everyone in Butte, it was simply "The Company." The Company seemed all-powerful, even omnipotent in our lives as it controlled every aspect of our community, including its water. The Company took while the people gave. It was how things operated in Butte, and even as a sixth grader, I grasped this concept. As The Company started showing signs of decline and job losses loomed I witnessed my friends being uprooted from their homes as their parents sought employment elsewhere. The community was experiencing the repercussions of The Company's struggles, and the effects were palpable.

"So this creek is dead forever then? There is nothing to be done?"

"Probably so, Raye. Probably so. I can't imagine a world where this creek will come back. There are tailings all throughout the Clark Fork too, which is sad because that river could be amazing, but even in the mainstem, there aren't many fish."

In 1983, my dad was likely right. There was nothing to be done for the long-dead Silver Bow Creek. On the day of his death, however, Silver Bow Creek was alive in a new way and home to a self-sustaining population of native west slope cutthroat trout.

When the fishing got slow, we'd go to the bank and pull rocks. My first entomology lessons were learned along riverbanks, with my father gleefully pulling up rocks to show me mayflies, caddisflies, and stoneflies. He would open the fly index and point to the flies that were intended to mimic each live animal, explaining that the wet flies mimic the juveniles and the dry flies mimic the adults. He discussed each insect's life cycle, reminding me that life is brief, and repeated his favorite line, "At least you are not a stonefly. Just think, you live most of your life as a juvenile, waiting for the magical day you become an adult. On that one day, you walk out of the water, crack open your juvenile body, dry your wings, take flight, find a mate, and die. Your entire adulthood over in a matter of hours. How would that be?" His laughter would ring out and I would roll my eyes. He would not be deterred during these moments, rather he'd just open the fly box and start to chatter away, commenting that maybe we needed to match the hatch better in order to catch our fish.

"People call this a hellgrammite. But it is a stonefly pattern. A real hellgrammite is a dobsonfly or alderfly and the fly pattern is different." My dad is pointing to what looks to me like a black ball of yarn on a hook, with two white points at the back and two at the front. He is pulling other flies and chatting away about what pattern matches what fly. I am mildly interested, but my teenage thoughts are on my friends and I am thinking, How long will we have to be here? He must sense my impatience as the next set of metaphors come rolling out of his mind. Again, I am patiently impatient, but the water feels good and I enjoy my father when he is happy and sharing his knowledge.

"I know you think that life is going too slow, that it will be forever before you are grown up and on your own. But that isn't true. Think about the river as a metaphor for time. Some days seem to pass in a flash, like the rapids. Others are slow and easy, almost standing still like the deep pools." His voice is sincere, and he looks me deeply in the eye, turning back to the fly box, settling the flies into their order and returning the box to the zip pouch on his vest.

"At your age, time seems eternal. You've just put your boat into the headwaters, if you will. If we measure our lives as we measure a float trip, imagine what it feels like to be nearing the end of the float, or nearing the end of the river itself, reaching the delta at the ocean. You cannot even see the end of your life. Your float is just beginning, you cannot see the delta on the near horizon, nor can you even imagine what it might be to be my age, about the middle of the float, let alone what it might be like to be old and ready for death, the delta in plain sight."

He continued, "At my age, it feels more like the rushing waters of spring. That time is passing quickly, and it's all you can do to hold on and stay steady in the water. Your life rushes past you in a blur if you aren't present. Pretty soon, your kids are grown and you are old. You wish for the deep pools, the slow easy days where time stands still and you can savor the moments of your life. You would rather that time pass slowly like the river flow in August, when it meanders like a lazy dog enjoying a slow walk. It's why I drag you out here to the river every summer, to stretch time, to enjoy our days to the fullest, to create memories, and if we are lucky, catch a fish."

It wasn't until I applied for a position with the Clark Fork Watershed Education Program (CFWEP) that I realized how much I had learned from my father during these slow fishing days. My first few days teaching were spent illustrating the importance of macroinvertebrates in the stream. Truth be told, I was relying totally upon my dad's teachings and listening to the other instructors, since I had never done stream assessments using the life in the stream as bioindicators. I used the observational skills he taught me to help my students ask questions like, "What is happening in this landscape?" My college degree, an award my dad never had, held nothing compared to his river teachings.

After my dad retired, he volunteered for our organization's field trips. The days were packed with fun and learning for the students of the Clark Fork Watershed. Each field trip consisted of several stations for students to learn about the condition of the stream through bioassessment. Of course, dad was assigned to the macroinvertebrate station. He had the immediate knowledge of identification, but the assessment strategy was new information and he jumped into it just as enthusiastically as the students, reporting back to me that Silver Bow Creek was still in a recovery phase.

During the restoration process of Silver Bow, our program had the opportunity to examine two sites along the stream, one damaged and one restored. The restoration was new, only in place a few years, and life was slowly beginning to come back. The macroinvertebrate life was not as diverse as we'd like to see it, nor were the riparian plants fully present, but compared to the Silver Bow Creek of my childhood, complete with sandy yellow beaches of tailings, the restored sections were beautiful. The downstream sections, in contrast, were exactly as they had been for a hundred years, devoid of life other than the most pollution-tolerant organisms.

The first time he spotted a stonefly on Silver Bow Creek, my dad had to immediately find me amongst the students collecting riparian plant data. He rushed over, joyous and exclaiming, "You have to come see it!"

Based on his energy and joy, I knew it must be something special. I moved myself into the crowd of seventh graders who were now gathered around one of our plastic tubs used for scooping and counting the insects. The kids were also exclaiming words like "Look at him! He's so cool! He looks like a dinosaur! Ah. Gross! What is that? Will it bite me?"

I peer into the tub and see a small golden stonefly. My (now-trained) eye recognizes that this particular stonefly is not very old, perhaps hatched out in the stream within the last year. I look at my father, who is beaming and has tears in his eyes. The tears make me laugh and I ask the students, "Do you know why Ray is so excited about this stonefly?"

They report to me that he thought this stream would be forever dead, that no life would ever be seen in this stream again, and that stoneflies are very sensitive to pollution; therefore, the presence of the stonefly is a good indicator that the restoration efforts are gradually improving the condition of the stream. Well done, dad, well done.

On our way home, my father is beaming and effusive with his commentary about how he underestimated Mother Nature. "It's astounding to me that with just a nudge, literally just removing the tailings and planting back a few willows, Mother Nature takes over and the stream is back!"

I start to correct him, to discuss the nuances of the restoration work and the billions of dollars that will be spent in this watershed, but decide to hold my comments for another day. His joy at witnessing life return to the creek fills my soul. Indeed dad, indeed—a little nudge is all it needed and here we are witnessing life return to this stream within a few short years. In fact, our CFWEP students were amongst the first to fish Silver Bow Creek during our annual fly fishing camp, another adventure for which my father volunteered and another day that brought tears to his eyes as one of the students he was teaching pulled a cutthroat from the stream.

The restoration and rebirth of our headwater creek was a topic of many conversations on my dad's front porch. He was so proud of me and the work that our organization did to carry the messages of hope and rebirth to the next generation. He often reminded me to be sure the kids knew that he never caught a fish there and his dad also never caught a fish there and it was a great privilege that they were now able to catch fish.

The challenges for this next generation are not of tailings and mine waste, but rather of climate change, drought, and overuse. During the field trips and lessons CFWEP presents, we discuss this generation's challenges and remind them that if you give back to the stream, it will give back to you, pointing to the nudge (as my dad called it) that our generation gave this river system. As part of our curriculum, we bring historical photographs for our students to witness the creek's condition before the restoration efforts. We highlight the remarkable transformation: the removal of tailings, the growth of willows and trees, and the revival of the once lifeless river.

My colleagues and I open each of our annual fly fishing camps with the story of rebirth and the restoration of the Clark Fork Watershed. We invite them to fish along Silver Bow Creek as our first stop during the week-long camp. I retell the story that my father wanted each of them to hear, that he and my grandfather never had the privilege of catching fish in this stream and that it is their honor to give back to the next generation, to ensure that kids at the camp and their future children will have a healthy and vibrant stream to fish.

We ask our students to give back in many ways throughout camp week, including participating in work projects such as helping Trout Unlimited plant willow plugs and water plantings that are newly installed along the banks of various streams. We carry garbage bags in case there is litter to collect, and we always say a word or two of thanks when we release a fish back to the stream and at the end of a fishing day. During the school year, we ask our students to also give back to the river. They create public service announcements to remind people to conserve and protect water. They participate in Earth Month, which is becoming a watershed-wide cleanup event. They bring the lessons learned in class home to their families and repeat the story of the Clark Fork to parents and siblings.

These lessons are not mine: rather, they are my father's, imparted to me during the many fishing days I spent with him. Give back. Say thank you when you release a fish. Remember your privilege. I hear his words spilling from my mouth to my students and I hope that they too will pass them along.

◦∞◦

The coroner and the police have left my dad's home. My family is still here and I am numb. The only thought in my mind is to go to the river, to seek solace and find my bearings. I tell everyone where I am headed. It is May and the river is high and their eyes betray a little worry. I am not going to wade, nor fish, nor float. I am simply going to the river. I will be fine, I tell them.

I drive to Melrose and turn into the fishing access that was one of our favorite spots. The green grass along the banks invites one to lay down and take a nap if the afternoon is too hot. On this day, the sun is shining and the breeze is gentle. Another time, it would be an absolute beauty of a day. The river is flowing along at its spring clip and I recognize that I would not likely wade across today if I were fishing, the water is too fast and powerful. Besides, today I do not have a fly rod. I have only my grief.

I walk over the bank, peel off my shoes and roll up my pants. I look down to find myself still dressed in the stretchy pants that I wear as pajamas. I laugh, again the inappropriate humor rising up in my chest. I forgot to change into regular clothes as I made my dash to the river. My face is swollen from tears and my hair is hastily pulled back in a ponytail. I don't care. I just want the river to wash this all away and when I pull my feet out, I want to drive home to find my father ready for breakfast.

I slide into the river and the slick rocks of the Big Hole are smooth beneath my bare feet. I swear I can hear his voice, "Take care now, those rocks are well polished from a thousand years of water." The cold water rushes about my ankles and I feel the power of spring runoff pulling at my legs. I wade a little deeper, wishing for the river to whisk me away too. How can I let you go? Tears fall, joining the waters, my tears now also being carried to the sea.

I breathe in and out, in and out, in and out. The river begins to soothe me, reminding me of the cycles of our lives. It is mid-May and the stoneflies are likely making their way closer to the banks, preparing for their emergence as adults. This too was a lesson from my father: that all things in the river have a cycle, that the river will return to its normal flow, that the spring torrent will not last forever.

This moment in my life is a spring torrent. I am being pushed and pulled, bounced along the bottom of the river like a stone. I too am being tumbled and smoothed by this spring cycle. I hear his words again, "Just pull your knees in and relax. You will be okay."

I look across the banks and notice that the river's flooding has deposited new cottonwoods along the gravel bars. New life is emerging there too. Without the floods, the cottonwoods cannot spread, their stands aging and not renewed. It is only during flooding, a time that stresses the parent trees, that the cottonwood seeds deposit, take root, and grow. The willows that just the season before were too dry, have their roots happily submerged in the high water and it looks like deer and moose along the riparian corridor have been munching on new willow shoots.

Memories of my first fish on a fly rod push themselves through my grief and tears. Dad bought me a 9-foot, 7-weight rod, a good beginner's package. Prior to the first fishing trip, we spent hours casting and learning how to present the fly. I approached the river, a Royal Wulff on the end of the line. I was ready and certain that on the first cast I would have a fish. Dad stood a little upriver of me, allowing me to be in the sweet spot in the hole. He is calling instructions from upstream and I hear his words, but my heart is hammering in my chest. I cast. It's okay. Not great, but it will do. The fly floats past me, I mend, no strike. I raise the line and cast again, better. Still no strike. I repeat and again, no strike.

I am focused and take a few steps to my right, moving my position to change where I am presenting. Dad, meanwhile, has moved up a bit and is now slightly out of sight, but I can still hear him reminding me to mend and keep the fly straight in front of me, pull in my slack. I cast and no strike, yet there are fish rising. What am I doing wrong? I start to feel the frustration build in my jaw when I snag the willows behind me on the back cast. I have to trudge back and retrieve my fly as I cannot pull it loose. I return to the spot and I hear dad, "Fish on!" I walk up to see him pull in a huge brown trout. He releases the trout, says thank you and tells me "Get back in the water, you can't catch a fish if you aren't in the water."

I return to the hole, cast again and again. No strike. I am certain there aren't any fish there. I reel in my line, trudge to the shore and wait for dad to come downstream. I am sitting on the bank and sulking when I hear his feet splashing through the shallow. He calls over to me, "What are you doing? Why aren't you fishing?"

I shrug and my twelve-year-old self is having an inner temper tantrum. He makes it look so easy and fun and I am just dumb. I can't do this right. I want my spinning rod back, thank you very much. Fly rods are stupid.

Dad comes over to the bank. "What's up, honey?"

"I don't want to fly fish. I don't catch anything. I want to use the panther martin and the spinning rod. Fly fishing is stupid." I have tears welling in my eyes and I can't meet his because I am ashamed of my impatience.

"Well. That's a choice you have, but you said you wanted to learn. You are learning. You just have to keep giving it some effort, that's all. I didn't catch a fish my first time either." We go through the basics of casting, the presentation of the fly, the mending, the slack, and the hookset when one strikes.

I am becoming impertinent. "I know, Dad! I have done all of that! Still no fish. I think they aren't in there."

"They are in there. Seems to me, you just aren't holding your mouth right."

A grin is sweeping under his mustache and I am annoyed. I splash back into the hole with the defiance and rage of a frustrated twelve-year-old girl. "Fine. You'll see. I do everything right and still no fish!"

Cast. Mend. Strike!

"Set the hook! Set the hook!" Dad is jumping up and down and rushing out to where I am standing. I lift my arm the way he showed me in the yard and I feel the energy of the fish on my line. I am laughing and he is yelling, "Reel, reel! Keep your tip up!"

He gets to me just as I have the little brown trout within reach. It is tiny compared to the fish he just landed, but it is mine and it is beautiful. Dad reaches down to show me how to release the fish. "What do you say?"

"Thank you, fish! Thank you! Thank you!" I exclaim as he uses the forceps to expertly pull the hook without hurting the fish. I watch it quickly dart back into the deep hole.

"What did you learn just now?" my father asks, knowing that his question extends beyond the technical aspects of casting, mending, or even catching fish.

I sheepishly answer, "You have to hold your mouth right."

"And that means what?"

"Be grateful." I look up at him with a tiny bit of shame for my frustration. He puts his arm around me and tells me he loves me no matter what, but in life, and in fishing, it's all about how you approach things.

The memory reminds me that water heals us. It provides all that is needed to sustain our lives, and in this moment, it whispers to me that just as the rushing waters of spring flow past, so too will the torrent of grief recede from my heart. I will breathe again without the ache in my chest. I will choose gratitude as I was blessed with a father who gave me the gift of river wisdom. I will cast a fly rod on another day and honor this man, but today I am here to seek solace, to renew my energy, to slow time and reflect upon my life. I stand in awe of the immense power of water, and to give thanks and reciprocity to the river and to the man who has shaped my life.

∞

Rayelynn Brandl currently serves as the Executive Director of the Clark Fork Watershed Education Program (CFWEP), which is committed to helping people understand the science of restoration within the United States' largest Superfund Complex. She is a dedicated educator, who aspires to use storytelling as a way to engage people in science by discovering the unique curiosities about their place on Earth.

FOURTEEN

THE ART OF RAISING KIDS ON THE BIG HOLE WITHOUT FISHING

John McKee

TIME IS MEASURED as a function of the speed of light. Dance, like a river, is never the same twice. You are literally made up of compounds created from the death of stars—said differently you are Stardust...and maybe the hardest thing to comprehend is that one need not fly fish to enjoy the Big Hole River.

If, in this moment, this concept were being presented to you in narrative form from the stage, the actor would, in that moment, see a room of conflicted and confused faces. Not fly fish on the Big Hole? What else would you do? What else can you do? The answer, simply, is to raise your kiddos on the river.

A few bends in the river, upstream of Pumphouse Bridge is the rock we call Jump Rock. Tabular, sloping down to the water on the upstream side and then rising to a couple-foot drop on the downstream side, Jump Rock has occupied a tradition in our family for 40 years.

This is where the complexities of appraising time disintegrate, and moments are simply measured by the expressions on a child's face. Coming upon the rock, a couple of hard back pulls on the oars to drop momentum and you gently bump the bow against that sloped upstream side.

The kiddos have been psyched for this moment for the last couple of minutes, perched in the front of the boat, knowing and not knowing what's coming at the same time. When that bump happens they're on the rock. Two quick pulls on the outside oar and current pulls you around into the downstream eddy.

The kiddos are now a few feet above your head, staring down at you, and with looks ranging from tempered fear to youthful grit. In that moment, they make their choice. Time slows down, the speed of light shifts from a known constant to a crisp flash-panned snapshot of stillness. Then, just as fast as it stopped, time resumes, and the outstretched arms of a flying child grab onto something, anything, as they crash down into the hypalon floor of the raft and the waiting arms of the people who love them.

After you pass under the Pumphouse Bridge, the Boulder Ballet presents a different natural Stonehenge. The dynamics of the river create an ever-changing ensemble, and the act of weaving, bending, and flowing with the music of the current is truly an art form.

On any single day, the line that worked yesterday doesn't show a path today. Imagine the soil around Stonehenge rising and falling day to day, the stones leaning over to the creep of time and then erected again by youthful archaeologists. The Boulder Ballet is the same. You flow under the bridge and are presented with an irrigation diversion to river-left. Don't run that. To run river-center, there are two available paths. The first path is between the left side diversion and the center rock. The second path is to the right of the center rock. The steps are clear; your ballet will start with this center rock.

From here on, the choreography for maneuvering your boat will differ only not by the day, but by the hour. Sometimes, by the minute. You will continue to navigate river-right, flowing over, dodging around, colliding with, and using the exposed rocks as you mirror the curves of the river of the canyon, and of the highway above that.

You'll spot an irrigation diversion river-right and you know you can't hold this right-side line for too long. The dance forces you to adjust again, accepting the prescience of knowing that the same river can never be floated twice. You shift to river-center and drift past this last diversion. The curtains on the Boulder Ballet have drawn to a close. The dance is over, and as you leave shifting river henge behind, your boat settles into the soft drift of the river.

Five calm minutes after the Boulder Ballet has drawn to a close the diversion dam sets up a man-made triple standing-wave that makes for one of the "Fang-Death Falls". When the kiddos were small, every little riffle was its own "Fang-Death Falls", easily lending itself to the incremental numbering system developed by my family of Fang-Death Falls 2, Fang-Death Falls 3, and Fang-Death Falls 4. Here, where the terrors of Fang-Death

Falls 1 are quickly forgotten in anticipation of Fang-Death Falls 2, the Stardust is handed off to the next generation as my kids are now experienced enough to run these riffles on their own.

On these three specific waves, when the kiddos were little, they were all the way in the front of the boat, faces over the pontoon, holding the outside cheat line and taking the waves straight on, splitting the water to the sides with their very bodies. As they grew, they began running this specific Fang-Death Falls, sitting in the pilot seat with a hovering Dad on the cooler, vigilantly ready to help with the oars. Finally, the Stardust of growing up on a river filters down, and you're watching from a second trailing boat as your son pushes into the third wave.

He's run this line in his mind a thousand times. He's already moved his passenger to the back of the boat. I know my son, he's about to do something hilarious and he wants me to see it. He's about to intentionally stand his 12-foot Maravia boat vertical, a trick of moving the weight to the rear of the boat and then pushing the third wave with just the right amount of forward oar. When that moment occurs he's crouching forward on the cooler's side, which is now horizontal because the boat is standing straight up. He's let a leashed oar loose so he can reach back and grab a strap on his unsuspecting passenger's PFD to keep them from pitching backward out of the boat and there on his face is a smile made possible by the Stardust that made him a river kid.

People speak of the moment that a fish strikes in lyrical verse and have only fleeting memories of the Big Hole River elsewise. Yes, there is an art to landing a fish, but so too, there is an art to raising children on the Big Hole without asking them to fish. That art, and its palette and hues, have been die-punched into my memories as innumerable moments at Jump Rock, the Boulder Ballet, and Fang Death Falls. Having never fished on the Big Hole I can honestly say that I don't feel as if I've missed a thing. I hope my kiddos and theirs feel the same way.

∽

John McKee first floated the Big Hole with his step-father in mid 1980 at five years old, right after moving to Butte, MT. Twenty-seven years later, he took his four-month-old son down the Big Hole for the first time and has spent summers of joy, splashing, and loving a river without ever having fished it....not once. When not on the river, John can be found in the high basins of the Tobacco Root mountains.

APPENDIX OF
DAD'S FISHING JOKES

∾

Publisher's note: Throughout this book are irresistible references to helpful and loving parents and grandparents of the masculine persuasion. I reckon there isn't a reader of this book who hasn't heard their dad or granddad tell one of these dumb jokes:

How can you tell a joke is a Dad joke?
When it becomes apparent.

Why can't you tell a joke while ice fishing?
Because it'll crack you up.

Where do fish sleep?
In a river bed.

What do you call a Dark Lord of Sith who likes to fly fish?
Darth Wader.

Why do ospreys eat fish?
Because donuts get soggy before they can catch them.

Larry's out fishin' on Wolf Lake and gets back to shore with a 4-foot lake trout. On the way to clean it, he runs into a guy who has a stringer with a dozen baby minnows. The guy looks at Larry's giant lake trout, turns to him, and says, "Only caught one, eh?"

Guy asks his buddy to sync his phone, so he throws it in the river.

Why did the trout leave the cult?
The were too sacri-fish-al.

What do you call a fish without an eye? fsh.

Why was the movie about fly fishing a box office flop?
Bad casting.

How many anglers does it take to change a light bulb?
One, but you should have seen the bulb, it must have been THIS big.

How many anglers does it take to change a light bulb?
Four, one to change the light bulb and three to brag about how big the old one was and about the one that they would have changed, but "it got away."

A guy's out fishin' on the North Saskatchewan.
After a while, another guy comes to join him.
"Had had any bites?" asks the second guy. "Yes, lots," replies the first one. "But they were all mosquitoes."

An Alberta old timer, talking of the good old days asks his grandson, "Have you ever hunted bear?"
His grandson: "No, but I've been fishing in shorts."

Fisherman: "What are you fishing for sonny?"
Boy: "I'm not fishing, I'm drowning worms."

A little kid is sittin' on a side road in Butte with a fishing line down the drain. Feeling sorry for him, and wanting to humor him, a lady gives him a buck, and kindly asks, "How many have you caught?" Kid says, "You're the 10th this morning."

What's the difference between a angler and a lazy student? One baits his hooks while the other hates his books.

How many Montanans does it take to go ice fishing? Four. One to cut the hole in the ice, and three to push the boat through.

Chad's out fishin' on the Big Hole, but doesn't catch a thing. On the way back home, he stops off at Albertsons. "I want to buy three trout," Chad says to the guy behind the counter. "Instead of putting them in a bag, throw them to me." "Why should I do that?" guy behind the counter asks. "So I can tell everyone that I caught three fish!"

Have you seen the new fishing website? No, it's not online yet.

What's the best way to watch the fishing channel? Live stream.

Why are fish smarter than humans? Ever seen a fish spend a fortune trying to hook a human?

What do romantic fish sing to each other? Salmon-chanted evening!

Where are most fish found?
Between the head and the tail!

What's the best way to catch a fish?
Have someone throw it at you.

Why don't trout make good detectives? Because they always get caught up in the case!

Why did the trout blush?
Because it saw the river's bottom!

Why are fish so gullible?
Because they fall for things hook, line, and sinker.

Why did the fly fisherman bring a ladder to the river?
Because he heard the fish were jumpin' out of the water.

And finally...
Mother to daughter advice. Cook a man a fish and you feed him for a day, but teach a man to fish and you get rid of him for all weekend.

DURVILE & UPROUTE BOOKS
DURVILE.COM

"Every River Lit" Series

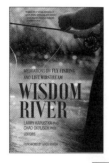

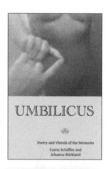

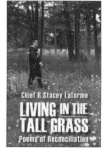

DURVILE & UPROUTE BOOKS
DURVILE.COM

"Ways of Light" Titles

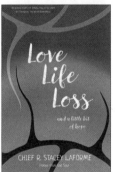

Durvile & UpRoute Books, a small-but-mighty Canadian indie press, publishes print books,
e-books, audiobooks, and rich multimedia for enhancement of meaning.
Our vision is to inspire authors and artists to bring new knowledge to the world.

ABOUT THE POETS
& ARTISTS

Doris Daley is an Alberta ranch girl whose love of wordsmithing has made her one of North America's favourite western poets, emcees, and western humorists. Doris's authentic, sparkling poetry has taken her to campfires large and small, to highways, roundabouts and gravel roads throughout the west, and to concert appearances with the Reno Philharmonic Orchestra and the Saskatchewan Opera Company.

Al (Doc) Mehl. With one foot in the past and one in the present, Doc weaves the history and the mystery of the West into his original "west-clectic" poetry and music. His poetry was publish, among many other places, in Vistas of the West. He lives in Diamond Valley, Alberta.

Tim Foster is a photographer, designer, and brand builder at Dose Media in Halifax, Nova Scotia.

Mike Forbister is a heavy equipment operator whose dad introduced him to fly fishing on the Oldman River at age twelve. He lives in Calgary, Alberta.

Tyler Rock is an instructor in the Glass program at the Alberta University of Art and an owner/artist at Firebrand Glass Studio in Diamond Valley, Alberta.

Rich Théroux is a genius talent at painting and drawing and is co-founder of Rumblehouse Gallery in Calgary, Alberta, along with his partner Jess Théroux.

ABOUT THE EDITORS & FOREWORD AUTHOR

Editor Larry Kapustka PhD is is an emeritus senior ecologist. He marvels at the intricacies of social-ecological systems and understands that we must be humble about what we think we know. Larry lives near Diamond Valley, Alberta.

Editor Chad Okrusch PhD is a professor of philosophy and communication at Montana Technological University in Butte, Montana. He is an award-winning singer and songwriter and has his second studio album underway, a follow-up to his debut album, Wisdom Road. Chad lives in Butte, Montana.

Foreword writer Greg Shyba is the CEO of the Ann & Sandy Cross Conservation Area in the foothills of Alberta. Prior to that, he was Executive Director of the Alberta Ingenuity Centre for Water Research and CEO of Trout Unlimited Canada. Greg has a passion for the outdoors with a particular love of fly fishing. Greg lives in Calgary, Alberta